INTERNET MARKETING BLUEPRINT FOR CHIROPRACTORS

Set your chiropractic practice apart with these new online marketing strategies

by

Steve Houston

INTERNET MARKETING BLUEPRINT FOR CHIROPRACTORS

Set your chiropractic practice apart with these new online marketing strategies

by Steve Houston

ISBN: 978-0-9852397-2-5

For more information, please visit:
http://NetCentricity.com

Contents

Preface

When this book was being written in early 2012, the United States was still struggling to emerge from the longest and most devastating economic recession in our nation's history. The Patient Protection and Affordable Care Act (PPACA) federal legislation signed into law by the 111th Congress was approaching a June ruling by the U.S. Supreme Court on the constitutionality of its "personal mandate" requirement, and the health care industry was in more than its usual state of flux, consternation and confusion.

It had also become clear from numerous studies that many consumers nationwide are delaying getting chiropractic, medical and dental care because of the recession-related reductions in household income and the loss of health insurance. It's possible that this fundamental shift from a "needs-based" model to a "wants-based" service delivery model may not change, or at best change slowly, even when the economy eventually begins to show sustained signs of recovery. This means that businesses dependent on consumer spending are being pressured to adapt to a more *value-driven* market environment.

The future outlook for the chiropractic industry is positive, though, because despite the temporary pressure on patient economics, chiropractic is still one of the most popular alternative health industries today. Patients have shown their willingness to invest in alternative care and natural products, and continue to obtain chiropractic treatment for back and neck pain, two of the most commonly treated medical conditions. Patients seeking chiropractic care fall mostly into the 31 – 50 and the 51 – 64 years age groups, the latter representing the huge, ripening demographic bulge referred to as "baby boomers". As such, chiropractic employment numbers are expected to increase about 18% over the next ten years.

However, in the here and now, the challenges remain. There are fewer patients with less disposable personal income...operating costs that continue to rise and insurance reimbursement rates that continue to fall...state and federal regulations that continue to discourage practice development and growth...local competition that continues to heat up...

Doesn't anything get any easier for a change?

Introduction

As if running a profitable chiropractic practice wasn't already difficult enough today, these two things called the "internet" and "internet marketing" come along to challenge most everything you thought you knew about how to market and develop your practice.

You might have had these thoughts cross your mind recently:

Now what? Websites I understand, sure, but internet marketing…and search engine marketing…what's that? And email marketing? Video marketing? Social media marketing? SEO? PPC? Mobile? SMS?

And what is this "reputation management" thing everyone is getting so concerned about?

Your head has every right to spin. Just keeping your practice open, profitable and growing right now poses more than enough challenges for you already. You intuitively, vaguely, understand that this "internet marketing" thing is important, but it's also a new technical lexicon and a different set of marketing practices that you're not familiar – much less comfortable – with yet.

It's my privilege to personally know a couple of chiropractic professionals, and I truly believe both of them pursued a career in chiropractic medicine because they had a sincere desire to help improve people's lives. But gauging by what I hear them say these days, neither ever imagined just how difficult it would become to deliver on that commitment. There are more challenges now than ever to running a successful business, despite the positive longer-term outlook for the chiropractic business.

However, because you need your practice to be successful, you know you can't just ignore issues like these when they arise. Instead, you wonder "*What am I going to do? How should I approach this? Where should I get started? How much am I going to have to learn? How much of my limited time will this consume? What will this cost me? What will it cost me if I don't - but my competitors do? Just what exactly should I do online to make my business grow?*"

Don't worry. In this book, I am going to tell you exactly WHAT you can do to leverage the power of the internet and make it work for you - in a language you can easily understand, and in a way that clearly illustrates the positive effects it will have on the growth prospects for your own chiropractic practice.

This book is *your* internet marketing blueprint - a custom business plan sharply focused on only the online strategies proven to be effective in helping private chiropractic practices flourish.

Who this book is for

This book *IS* for you if:

- You're a new chiropractor or just need to finally get started marketing your chiropractic practice online.
- You have an established private practice and want to attract more patients to it.
- You already have a website and other online marketing assets but they're not giving you the results you expected.
- You need some qualified help developing and implementing an effective online marketing plan for your practice.
- You want to stand out as a leader in the chiropractic field that you've chosen to practice in.

This book *IS NOT* for you if:

- You're a do-it-yourselfer. This is a strategic online marketing program to help guide your business development, not a detailed "how to create a website" tutorial.
- You are perfectly content with the current size, profitability, and long-term growth potential of your chiropractic practice.
- You will be closing or selling your practice.

I'm assuming that as a successful chiropractic practitioner and business owner, you are already far too busy **managing** your practice to be able to devote any amount of time to learning all the mechanics of this new, rapidly evolving, and highly specialized internet marketing technology. Therefore, this book will not attempt to teach you how to implement the technical aspects of it yourself.

Rather, it will provide you with a high-level, comprehensive online marketing plan that cuts through all the techno-speak and lays out, in simple terms, exactly which steps a private chiropractic practice should take to effectively market itself online and, even more strategically, position itself for long term success.

Once you have finished reading this book, you will be:

- able to more clearly envision your own high-level online marketing strategy that would best support your business;
- well informed and comfortable discussing strategy and technical requirements with the qualified internet marketing consultant of your choosing;
- better positioned to recognize the successful impact your new online marketing program will have on your practice.

This book will help you carry on a well-informed conversation with a qualified internet marketing consultant about the strategies that would make the most sense for your own practice. Implemented correctly, your custom program will attract new patients to you, help differentiate your practice from your competitors, and improve your ability to continue providing high quality, cost effective chiropractic care to your community.

So let's get started.

CHAPTER 1 - Internet Inception

In the beginning

It helps, I think, to first briefly put this game-changer called **the internet** into some kind of historical perspective because its importance simply cannot be overstated. Just as the invention of the steam engine in the nineteenth century catapulted America from being primarily an agricultural economy into becoming *the* global industrial power, and Henry Ford's assembly line in the twentieth century revolutionized manufacturing by introducing the concept of mass production, the invention of computers and their connectivity via the internet has since then fundamentally transformed our nation's economy into one based primarily on the free flow and widespread availability of information.

The internet has been so radically transformative because of the speed and ease with which it allows information to be accessible to everyone. Starting out in 1969 as a data "packet-switched" networking platform between the United States Defense Advanced Research Project Agency (ARPA) and various universities and research centers, the internet grew and metamorphosed itself into a more business-centric network infrastructure over time as networking equipment not only became more powerful but also cheaper to build and operate on a broad commercial scale.

The layer of the internet that the great majority of us operate in – the World Wide Web (www), or likewise anything beginning with the **http://** protocol - has become a highly efficient and inexpensive transactional channel that has insinuated itself into most people's everyday lives.

What do Citizens do on the Internet?

Check e-mail	94%
Search	87%
Product research	78%
Get news	75%
Pass time	72%
Buy a product	66%
Social network	61%
Search "how to" info	59%
Rate product or service	32%

Source: "Digital Marketing Budget Trends for 2012", 6smarketing.com, October 2011

Netcentricity as a key characteristic

When applied specifically in a commercial sense, the inherent flexibility of the internet has greatly increased the number of communication "channels" businesses can use to not only reach out and market through but interact with their customers worldwide.

> Both asynchronous and real-time, omnidirectional, media-diverse, cost-effective interconnectivity between you, your customers, and business colleagues...designed to readily facilitate online transactional activity…and implemented wherever it "makes sense" for your specific business niche…is what I refer to as **netcentricity**.

Customers themselves are increasingly demanding that the businesses they patronize must demonstrate some expected degree of "netcentricity" as a pre-condition for engagement with them. The internet has liberated the consumer from the traditional one-way B2C marketing model, now empowering them to engage with businesses in the kinds of online environments that they feel most comfortable in. Businesses are now having to choose whether or not they'll follow those potential - and existing - clients in those same arenas.

Smart businesses go where their customers are

The qualities that this enhanced degree of netcentricity offer have also helped level the playing field for businesses of all sizes, particularly because the cost of entry has been effectively removed as an obstacle for even the owner of the smallest business.

For example, a small chiropractic practice consisting of just one chiropractor – equipped with an easily findable, informative, and patient-engaging website – can now compete online against larger chiropractic practices who have significantly more marketing dollars to spend.

And when that same small practice applies some additional relevant and net-centric internet marketing strategies to its overall business plan, it can dramatically increase its competitive capabilities even further.

The emergence of internet marketing

Internet marketing emerged in the early 1990s as the internet itself exploded onto the scene. Also referred to as online marketing or web marketing, IM became a way to promote and sell products and services over the web in an increasingly cost effective manner.

Email, video, social media sites like Facebook, Twitter, and LinkedIn, SMS (text) messaging, mobile webs, mobile applications, QR codes, geo-marketing, and other net-centric technologies that ride the internet backbone came into their own as legitimate marketing devices. When smartly implemented, they have clearly proven to be effective in helping build positive relationships between businesses and the consumers they market goods and services to.

Along with these new online applications came a veritable flood of tools, metrics, and marketing devices that had never existed before. They empowered people to either self-market their own businesses or contract with a new breed of marketers called online marketing consultants to handle it instead for them. They also gave business owners new, accurate ways to measure the effectiveness of their online advertising efforts. Clicks and conversions (into customers) can be measured more readily, and the ROI on a company's online marketing spend is now a fairly straightforward calculation. Traditional marketing devices like direct mail and Yellow Pages ads still don't provide those kinds of near instantaneous and granular metrics that online marketers and net-centric business owners now have at their disposal.

The relevance and effectiveness of these new applications like video marketing, SMS marketing, and mobile marketing in a particular business niche will vary, but in general, the more of them that can be woven into one's marketing plan, the more they will help you achieve that connectedness, that appropriate degree of netcentricity that your business needs to envelop itself within to remain competitive.

And at the end of the day when you look at how well your online marketing assets have supported your business, you should be able to clearly see that not only have they brought you new clients, but that your marketing program has more than paid for itself in doing so.

Customer Lifetime Value (CLV)

Before we go any further, it would help to briefly acknowledge the issue of customer lifetime value. Successful business owners understand that the cost of acquiring a new customer significantly exceeds the cost of retaining an existing customer. They also know that the longevity and profitability of their enterprise is dependent upon repeat business from a loyal, high-quality clientele. Thus it becomes important not only to attract the right kind of new clients to your business, but to also nurture and maintain the relationships you already have with your current clients.

Understanding your patients' CLV to your practice is extremely useful in a number of ways:

- It helps quantify just how valuable (in dollars) the relationships you have with your patients are.
- It can help you shape your marketing program by better understanding the ROI of the various marketing methods used for customer acquisition.
- It can also help you determine the types of services you should be providing that maximize your practice's earning potential.

There are a number of free, easy-to-use CLV calculators available online that you can use to help with your planning. I'd suggest you familiarize yourself with one of them when you become more serious about planning and implementing a new online marketing program for your chiropractic practice.

Internet marketing is relationship marketing

It's important, at this point, to hammer home the fact that the traditional marketing practices that businesses have followed for years – particularly as used in the professional / chiropractic service verticals - are undergoing a fundamental devaluation not only in the ultimate effectiveness of their message, but also in the broader sense of how they're viewed relative to your own company's marketing strategy.

Most of the traditional marketing methods such as outbound telemarketing, direct mail, TV and radio media buys, printed Yellow Pages directories, and newspaper and magazine advertising are all predicated on the same underlying approach – one-way communication. Using any or all of these channels, you essentially "pushed" your message out to your targeted prospects.

In the "old" days when businesses blasted out these advertisements, one could reasonably count on some number X recipients, out of the hundreds or thousands you initially targeted, responding favorably to your message by either walking through the front door of your business or calling to make an appointment.

However, many marketing strategies that worked reasonably well in the past are simply not working as well in the present, and a reasonable person might expect to see them become even less relevant moving further into the future.

Granted, none of these traditional methods have completely lost their effectiveness, and a strong argument can and should be made for the proven wisdom of combining the most relevant of both online AND offline marketing methods into a coherent plan for your own business. But the inescapable truth of today is that legacy media simply are not "converting" potential clients into actual clients at the same rates they used to. Businesses are beginning to awaken to this fact and many are making adjustments to where their future marketing dollars will be invested.

Digital Marketing Spend (2012 estimates)

41% of companies state they would reduce print media investments

64% will invest more in social media on their blogs & product reviews

64% plan to increase budget for SEO (search engine optimization)

70% plan to increase social media investments

Source: "Digital Marketing Budget Trends for 2012", 6smarketing.com, October 2011

As the statistics above illustrate, significant portions of corporate marketing budgets are being shifted away from legacy marketing systems into digital marketing strategies in order to be more responsive to the challenges – and opportunities - that an increasingly net-centric world poses for business.

Today's consumer calls the shots

Again, this is because the balance of power in the **Provider – Consumer** relationship has changed. Not only have consumers had such an ever-widening variety of products and services to choose from, but the inexpensive and easy-to-use communication technologies now available provide them an unprecedented level of access to information and dialogue that are forcing companies to engage with them in new, uncharted ways. Chiropractic medicine is no different as it becomes an increasingly consumer-driven business fueled by more and more powerful communication channels that facilitate even more choice.

Today's consumers now have instant "one click" access to retail websites where they can easily compare vendors and product prices...

...and can visit review websites where, before choosing whether to patronize your business or not, they can read other people's candid (and sometimes unflattering) comments about it...

...and now have the ability to make much more informed choices about where they spend their money than they ever did before.

One can clearly see, then, that the emergence of a different marketing dynamic – *one of active online engagement, rather than just one-way telling and selling* – has become the new 21st century marketing mindset for any business that wants to flourish.

The marketing game has changed for everyone, and that includes chiropractic professionals. Reliance on the more dignified, low key, word-of-mouth referral process for bringing in new clients just isn't adequate anymore. Actively going to where the best potential clients can be found – and becoming comfortable using new channels and methods to get there – has become the new marketing imperative.

The question then becomes: Who will adapt more quickly and effectively – you or your competitors?

So, as a concerned business owner who wants their chiropractic practice to grow and prosper even during these turbulent economic times, where should one begin to take advantage of this new internet marketing world?

With your website.

CHAPTER 2 - The Humble Website

Before going any further, and at the risk of overstating the obvious, I'll go ahead and say it. If you're not online – **and findable** - when potential patients are searching for your practice, chances are they will not even know you exist and will instead patronize competing chiropractic professionals who do have an easier-to-find website and other online marketing assets for their practices.

Many people now tend to overlook the importance of a well-designed website because of the dizzying array of online applications that have so quickly and recently emerged to overshadow it. Yet, the website remains arguably the most important online marketing asset a business can possibly have in its inventory.

So, if you don't already have one, get one. You need it because your website is a virtual, online representation of your physical brick-and-mortar storefront. And people are living more of their lives in that virtual cyberspace.

Your website is your own advertising billboard somewhere out along the vast information superhighway called the internet where large numbers of people - potential customers - drive daily searching for it.

It won't quickly disappear into the recycle bin like direct mail advertising, newspaper and magazine printed ads, and other types of one-shot, one-way marketing devices do. Pay the inexpensive web hosting and maintenance fees to keep it up and running and your website is always there, 24 hours a day, 7 days a week. Always open, always trying to make your new visitors feel welcomed.

And best of all, you own it. You control it, you determine the content that gets posted on it, and you can make it as functionally sophisticated – or as brain-dead simple – for your visitors as you want. Once traffic arrives at your website, its job is to then help you convert them to paying customers.

.

Your website is one of your most valuable online assets and should be positioned as the centerpiece of your online marketing strategy. All the other building blocks that you may choose to implement in your online marketing strategy are secondary and complementary to this foundational piece.

> The main website of a business is frequently referred to as the "money site" because from it, directly or indirectly, all money flows.

Your domain name is important

No business website would be complete (or would exist, for that matter) without a domain name (e.g., www.chiropractoronline.com). Domain names are registered from domain registrars ("leased" is probably a more apt descriptor) in annual increments, and generally cost between $10 – 25 per year.

Without going into too much technical detail here, there are several important factors to consider when choosing a domain name for your chiropractic practice.

First, make it as easy as possible for people to read and spell your domain name. It will also be easier for them to remember.

Second – and only as a general rule of thumb - the shorter the domain name, the better. The fewer the keystrokes you force people to enter, the less chances there are of typos and the quicker it is to key in and submit.

However, that having been said, don't be shy about including some relevant "keywords" in it, even at some expense to its overall length. The search engines do give some credit for finding relevant keywords in your domain name. **Keywords** are what the search engines use to return relevant search results to people who are searching for something using those same terms. (There will be more on keywords in the next section.)

If you intend to market your practice as a "brand", then use the brand name in the domain name. Some examples might be:

- www.acmefamilychiropractic.com
- www.JohnSmithChiropractor.com

The use of hyphenated domain names is discouraged simply because they add unnecessary complexity and no value.

Last but not least, always reserve a domain name that uses the **.com** extension. Originally intended to designate commercial websites, the .com (dot com) extension is by far the most used domain type and the easiest for people to remember.

> Your goal is to strike the right balance between memorability, length, and keyword relevance when choosing a domain name.

Your website must inspire K-L-T

Consumers have become increasingly sophisticated about making purchasing decisions using the internet, and more frequently than not make judgments about what to buy – and who to buy it from – by leveraging all of the information readily available to them online.

Savvy customers are informed customers, and a well-designed business website will provide many of the answers to questions potential customers will have about a company. For every business, there are several key steps in establishing a profitable relationship with them, by virtue of this simple formula:

- Helping them get to **KNOW** you
- Makes it easier for them to **LIKE** you
- And once they like you, they'll find it easy to **TRUST** you.

This **K-L-T factor** is perhaps THE most critical element of any successful internet marketing program. It is a widely recognized marketing tenet around which a variety of actions should be taken to see it materially implemented.

So just how does one go about establishing one's business as a trustworthy partner using a website as their primary vehicle? Here are the four most important characteristics any effective business website will need to have to earn a potential client's trust:

1. It will have free, valuable content that will educate and entertain its visitors. Recent articles, whitepapers, case studies, chiropractic news, self-help info, and any other types of interesting – and usable - content related to the chiropractic niche are all great candidates for your website. The "stickier" (i.e., more interesting) your website is, the more your visitors will want to return and spend more time on it. This is generally how they'll first find you and this is where the relationship usually starts. (But you can overdo it. Too much content crammed into a webpage will overwhelm a first-time visitor and they will simply click away.)

2. It will have the ability to subconsciously legitimize your professional authority in your chosen business niche. The quality, relevance and freshness of content that you post on it, how professional your website looks, and the ease with which your visitors can navigate it are all important psychological elements that project a professional image to potential clients and help earn their trust.

3. It will have mechanisms for them to use to easily engage you through. These frequently take the form of a basic Contact page through which visitors can send you questions or comments, or your prominently posted phone number. Smart business owners use their websites as a channel to regularly interact with their customers, as engagement is now the main underlying strategy of effective internet marketing.

4. Many chiropractic websites provide information about their chiropractic services, policies, and procedures, but few go into enough detail profiling the chiropractors themselves. A full web page on your website should be devoted to each chiropractor in the practice listing their professional qualifications, specialties, achievements, personal information, education and training, and whatever else people look for in order to better get to know someone. It's difficult to overstate the importance of the KLT factor, particularly as it pertains to choosing someone to whom you'll entrust your personal health.

Because of all the turbulence in the medical care industry these days, edgy consumers are looking for whatever information they can find in order to make the best-informed choices. A full-page, well-written biography on each of the chiropractic staff in your practice will help put a human face on them, increase their likability and authority, and help personalize the relationship you want to develop with them.

Design your website for new visitors

Numerous studies have shown that a typical new visitor to a website will determine within the first five seconds of landing on it whether or not it's worth their time to remain there. Remember, they probably came to your site through a search engine or another link, and they're only one click away from abandoning your site for one of the other myriad of sites they can choose from.

With that in mind, you will want to have the home (main) page of your website designed in a way that first grabs your visitors' attention. It should also make it easy for them to find what they're looking for by providing easy-to-follow navigation links to other pages on your site.

There are also several best-in-class design elements – each working to achieve your different marketing objectives - that have been proven over time to work best in influencing visitors to take a specific action you wanted them to take while on your website. Later on the book we'll cover these highly effective tactics that are very important for building positive, profitable relationships with your customer base.

Ideally, when your website is being designed, the designer should also attempt to view it through the perspective of someone who isn't familiar with your company and may not even know what your company offers. One way to do this objectively is through the use of an "avatar", or fictional model, of your typical chiropractic patient and all the demographic traits you think they possess. The more complete this profile is, the more effectively it can be used for physical website layout, ongoing content development, and general marketing strategy orientation.

Choose a development platform thoughtfully

There are several applications commonly used as website platforms today and each brings its own advantages and disadvantages to the discussion.

HTML (hypertext markup language) has been the traditional coding platform for most websites since the advent of the internet. HTML provides web developers with highly customizable control of website design, but the relative complexity of the code and the increasing scarcity of HTML-literate website developers are combining to make HTML less attractive as the leading design platform it once was.

Adobe's **Flash** technology is another popular design platform typically used for higher-end websites. Vibrant graphics and richer-looking design are some of the visible hallmarks of Flash sites, but those attractive features are offset by some significant negatives that Flash technology poses for website owners.

Large Flash sites are slower to load on most web browsers (and the search engine Google is now penalizing slow-loading websites). Also, Flash will not display on Apple devices like iPads and iPhones that use the iOS operating system. Flash-based websites are also significantly more difficult and expensive to update, optimize and maintain for the search engines.

CMS (content management systems) like WordPress, Drupal, and Joomla have most recently become the favorite development platforms for many website designers. WordPress, in particular, is attractive because it is "open source" blogging software (i.e., free to use even for commercial purposes), easy to set up and manage, and can be customized using any number of free or low-cost theme templates and plug-ins that can provide the additional functionality that a business website needs. (Google also favors WordPress-based websites from an SEO standpoint. As an online content management system, its architecture makes it easy for Google's "spider" programs that crawl the internet to index any WordPress web pages they find in its vast database.)

It can cost between several hundred to several thousand dollars to develop a custom business website, primarily depending upon the type of technology used, how much functionality the website is equipped with, and its overall size. Flash sites are currently the most expensive to build and maintain; CMS-based sites are at the other end of the cost spectrum; and HTML-based sites generally fall somewhere in between.

A quick word about blogs

CMS-based **blogs**, or web logs, are generally characterized as being personal journals posted online by so-called bloggers who use them as virtual pulpits from which they can share their thoughts with the masses. They are also another common form of website. Because of the informality that blogs usually convey, though, I would suggest avoid using a blog's typical "look and feel" for your business website. Again, you are trying to earn your prospects' trust by projecting a certain formality or authority; in my opinion, blogs demonstrate neither very well.

Recommendation

With that said, **I would suggest using the WordPress blogging software** for your chiropractic practice's web platform, but customize it so it looks like a formal HTML-based website and not just some free, available-to-everyone blogging software.

Most web designers themselves consider WordPress to be the most robust, inexpensive to maintain, and easy to update type of online website publishing environment available today. You will also want to consider, as part of your overall SEO strategy, having more than one website for your chiropractic practice, and certainly if you have offices in other cities. The WordPress platform scales well for multiple networked business sites.

Provide a mobile-friendly version of your website

Although other "mobile marketing" applications will be covered in more detail in a later chapter, it's a good idea to briefly address "mobile web" here as it relates to the primary website of a business.

- "Mobile" internet users are expected to outnumber "desktop" PC internet users by 2014.

- By 2013, approximately 60 million Americans will be using internet-enabled smartphones.

- Half of all **local** searches are performed on smartphones, tablets and other mobile devices.

Having itself made significant investments in mobile technology, Google fully understands that mobile search will be the next significant frontier for search delivery. It also knows that the physical user experience of mobile search is different than search performed on a desktop PC or laptop.

Remember, Google's main concern about their customers' search experience is that their search results are relevant. Web pages deemed to be the most relevant by Google are rewarded with higher rankings in their SERPs, and higher rankings drive more prospect traffic to your website.

When viewed within this context of relevancy, here are some things that Google thinks web designers should pay attention to if they want to deliver a good (i.e., relevant and easy) mobile search experience. For now, Google is applying these best-practice standards only to websites of companies running AdWords campaigns:

- The website needs to load quickly on mobile devices. Delays are irritating and large files sizes can incur additional monthly data expenses for the smartphone owner.
- It avoids using Flash technology.
- Content is easily readable without having to stretch, zoom or enlarge the display area of their smartphone screen.

Although software exists to "squeeze" a web page (originally designed to be viewed on a large computer monitor) down to the size of a smartphone display, it usually renders the result unreadable. This commonly used approach should always be avoided.

The best solution is to have two separate websites. Your primary .com (commercial) site would contain all of the main content and would be available for visitors with larger PC displays, and a lightweight secondary .mobi (mobile) site would present a more condensed version of it to mobile visitors. Special code applied to your primary .com website can determine which visitors to it are on mobile devices and would then automatically re-direct them over to the .mobi website.

Recommendation

Yes, deploy a mobile-friendly website as an important complement to your primary website. It will become another important feature of your practice's overall online marketing plan as mobile search continues to become more commonplace. It becomes even more of a necessity if the type of chiropractic medicine you practice has emergency, on-call, or "immediate response" elements to it.

Fig. 2.1 – Your primary and mobile websites

CHAPTER 3 - Search Engines 101

When someone searches for something online, the search engine takes the search term that was entered and references it against a massive database where all of the web pages currently known to exist on the internet have been found and indexed by keyword. It then looks for documents that match those keywords and returns a list of what it thinks are the most relevant web pages to the searcher.

No one knows exactly how many unique web pages exist out there today but Google acknowledged passing the one-trillion-unique-pages-indexed milestone back in 2008. Since then they've gone on to estimate that several billion more web pages are being added to the web every day.

The key concept to understand here is relevancy. A search engine's overarching objective is to return only the most relevant results to its search clients, quickly and accurately. Google considers a multitude of factors in its highly complex, constantly evolving, ultra-top-secret search algorithm when determining relevancy. Because the concept of relevancy is so important to this discussion, you'll be reading quite a bit more about it later.

So as you can see, Google, Yahoo!, Bing, and any number of other lesser search engines on the web have quite a formidable task to accomplish – to be able to pick your particular needle out of a one trillion page+ haystack. And to do it accurately hundreds of millions of times every day for their users.

Relevancy = Visitors

When your practice has a well-designed sticky website **that searchers can easily find,** you can expect a certain number of those visitors to later turn into paying customers - new patients who will actually call to make chiropractic appointments and then walk through your office's front door.

The higher your website is listed in the search engine's results pages (SERPs), the more visitor traffic it should get. On average, the top 3 websites listed on page 1 of Google SERPs receive about half of all the visitors.

There are a number of steps, then, that should be taken to help Google recognize your own website's relevancy and increase the probability that searchers will see your website listed on the first page of Google's search results.

Enter search engine optimization, aka SEO

Entire shelves of books have been written about this arcane science of search engine optimization, so I won't make an effort here to explain its many technical subtleties or how to go about doing it. You should leave that to the experts. I will attempt in this chapter, though, to paint a high-level view of the SEO discipline for you, explain how important it is to your overall internet marketing strategy, and show you how a well-crafted SEO campaign can pay for itself many times over when implemented properly.

Keyword selection

Choosing keywords that searchers will use to try to find your business with is a critical component of getting the right visitors (i.e., targeted traffic) to your website. As the business owner / subject matter expert, you play an important part in that selection process. You probably have a good idea which keywords prospective patients would use to try to find your chiropractic practice.

Your internet marketing consultant has access to a number of web-based tools and can also help you select the keywords best suited for your particular business niche and marketing objectives. The Google Adwords Keyword Tool, for instance, will show the average number of times a certain keyword or keyword phrase was used for search last month, whether they were local or global searches, and other closely related keyword variations.

> In general, the more frequently a keyword is used for search - and for which your website is optimized - the more traffic it will attract.

Organic traffic vs. paid traffic

There are two basic types of search traffic that Google can send to your website – the results of "organic" (free) search, and traffic generated by using paid advertisements through Google's AdWords program. Google and the other search engines display both types of results in different areas of their SERPs.

In this chapter, we'll be discussing only organic search and the actions that should be taken to fully leverage the power of free organic search. Paid advertising, also referred to as PPC (pay-per-click) will be discussed briefly later on in another chapter as yet another effective traffic generation method that may be an appropriate element in your own marketing program.

On-page vs. off-page SEO

Search engine optimization takes place at both the micro and macro levels – on your website, and then on every other online property you own outside of your website.

"On-page" optimization involves developing your site in a way that both its content and structure contribute to making it search engine friendly. Just as you want each web page to be attractive to visitors, you also want each web page to be attractive to the search engines through the strategic use of carefully chosen keywords within the content of your web pages.

Most websites consist of multiple web pages united by a common theme. Google and other search engines rate each individual page – not the entire web site - for relevancy against the search term used to look for it. Each web page on your site, then, should be optimized using a different, but related, keyword phrase or keywords to increase the likelihood of each of your web pages being found.

Depending upon the particular type of chiropractic you perform, some of the keywords used on your website's various pages may include:

Website homepage	Chiropractic page	Massage Therapy page	Rehabilitation page
family care	Joint manipulation	reduce muscle spasm	Ultrasound therapy
general chiropractic Austin*	Flexion / distraction	trigger points	interferential current

**Note the keyword including the word "Austin". Using "geo-targeted" keywords is a powerful technique that helps narrow down overly broad search results to only those relevant to the searcher's physical location.*

Each web page should be optimized around one primary - but no more than two total - keywords or keyword phrases. Any more than two might confuse the search engines who might penalize your web pages with relatively bad search engine rankings.

Other key factors Google considers in its on-page relevancy algorithms include:

- The page title's use of keywords
- Keyword usage in the page's metadata tags
- Keyword density, location and embellishment within the page content
- Proper use and sequencing of H1, H2 and other markup tags
- Use of contextually-related keywords in your content (LSI or latent semantic indexing)
- Using keyword-related file names and alternate text for images
- Proper placement and use of on-site navigational keyword-rich "anchor text" links

> Whether you provide your own website's content or hire someone to create it for you, make sure to pay close attention to these critical SEO elements from the very beginning of your website's design process.

"Off-page" optimization describes another important SEO strategy that involves helping popularize your practice's site by maximizing the number of high quality external websites linking back to it.

Google assumes that the more incoming links from other websites a web page has pointing to it, the more popular and relevant that webpage is, thus the higher search engine ranking it deserves. Each link to your website is viewed, in effect, as a "vote" for your website. The more votes it captures from other sources (particularly high-authority websites), the more relevant it is, so helping increase your website's "link popularity" is an important facet of any off-page SEO strategy or campaign.

There is a wide variety of internet resources from which to link back to your practice's website and give it an added boost of relevance and authority. Some of the most powerful sources of inbound links include:

- Articles posted to high-quality article directories like EzineArticles.com
- Guest content published on personal and commercial blogs

- Links from highly authoritative sites, .edu sites, and .gov sites
- Commercial press releases about your business
- Business directories like Google Places and YP.com
- Video sharing sites like YouTube and Vimeo
- Signature links in comments posted in discussion forums
- Social media sites including Facebook and LinkedIn
- Social bookmarking sites such as Delicious and Diigo

An effective SEO strategy for your practice will include the development and implementation of link schemas for both on-page and off-page optimization in addition to the organic link growth that will also occur. The actual work of off-page link building through article marketing, RSS feed syndication, guest blogging, forum commenting, social bookmarking, and other related activities should be undertaken in a deliberate manner that mimics the natural growth of inbound links. Off-page optimization is an ongoing, labor-intensive process and is another ideal function to contract out to your internet marketing consultant.

Change is constant online

Nothing online is completely static. Google and the other search engines are constantly modifying their search algorithms to improve the search experience for their users, just as your competitors are always making adjustments to better optimize their websites for higher Google rankings than yours.

So when you publish a website for your practice, please accept the fact that you're also making an important commitment to an ongoing SEO program needed to keep your own website relevant, highly visible – and profitable. You're also going to find it important to regularly post fresh content on your website to help keep it attractive not only to your visitors, but ultimately to Google too.

Recommendation

A well-designed ongoing SEO program will keep your website ranking highly in the search engines, making you stand out above the other chiropractic practices you are in competition with. Find a knowledgeable SEO consultant that can build and manage this important internet marketing program for you.

If you already have a website and it's not ranking on the first page of Google, then you need to consider pursuing a similar approach to make it competitive again. There's no point in having a website unless prospective patients can actually find it when they're searching for your type of business, a chiropractic practice, to schedule an appointment with.

FIG. 3.1 - SEARCH ENGINES SEND TRAFFIC TO YOUR WEBSITE WHERE YOU TRY TO CONVERT THEM INTO CUSTOMERS

CHAPTER 4 - Google AdWords PPC advertising

Pay-per-click (PPC) advertising is what Google uses to generate most of its billions of dollars in annual corporate profits. Businesses advertising online have flocked to its AdWords program in droves because it has proven that it can be a very effective way to drive significant amounts of targeted "click through" traffic to their websites.

Google's PPC AdWords program is also based on the keyword search model and uses an auction-based system to determine placement of paid ads on its SERPs. ("Sponsored" AdWords ads are placed at the top and/or bottom of a Google search results page and also down the right-hand side of the page. "Organic" - free - search results make up the main middle section of the page.)

Advertisers bid for the keywords that they want to use in their ads, and the bid they lock in determines how much they'll pay Google each time someone sees and physically clicks on one of their AdWords ads, which redirects them to their business website.

Their bid also determines how frequently their ads are rotated onto the page during a 24-hour period, and also to whom the ad is presented (geo-targeting again at work here).

PPC campaigns can be set up, for the most part, to run automatically. However, PPC marketing experts understand that there's quite a bit more to running a successful campaign than that, and frequent, hands-on active involvement is the key to running successful campaigns. Constant tweaking of your ads' keywords and overall content is important to finding the version that resonates – and converts - the best with consumers.

A simple one-word change in an ad's title can increase its effectiveness immensely. PPC campaign managers routinely run what are called "split tests" in which different ad versions are published concurrently to see which earns the higher conversion rates, making adjustments to wording, graphics, layouts, etc., as they test. It's an ongoing process requiring hands-on involvement but it's also the best way to maximize the return from your PPC budget.

PPC costs for the business owner can run anywhere from a couple of pennies per click all the way up into tens of dollars per click, depending upon the business niche and degree of competition within that niche. For many of the most competitive keywords in the chiropractic field, PPC costs can be fairly significant. For example, bidding on the keywords "chiropractic adjustment" and "chiropractic neck adjustments" is currently running about six dollars per click.

Recommendation

Perhaps. Many chiropractors commonly use Google AdWords to drive potential patients to their websites. Discuss the costs and benefits of running a PPC campaign with your online marketing consultant to see if it makes sense for your practice. I would suggest you first begin with a formal organic SEO campaign concentrating on stimulating free search traffic to your website. In some niches where competition for high rankings isn't as acute, free organic traffic may provide you with all the traffic you want.

However, in the more competitive niches where competition is keener, a modest pay-per-click campaign may very well be a cost-effective complement to your organic (free) SEO program. Again, knowing your typical patient's CLV will help you decide which course(s) of action are going to offer you the best chances for the best ROI on your marketing spend. Set aside an initial budget to build a trial AdWords campaign, and have your consultant test and tweak it until it becomes consistently profitable.

CHAPTER 5 - Google Places, et al

Literally millions of searchers use Google Maps every day to find local businesses, and a free listing for your own business will make it easier for them to find you too. When potential clients use Google Maps to search for local information, they'll find useful data like your business address, hours of operation, types of payment accepted, photos or videos you may have posted about your business, and the all-important link back to your primary website which helps boost its authority.

Frequently a Google Places listing for your business will already exist when you first look and you can claim it using their mail verification system. Once claimed, it affords you the valuable opportunity to update it with quite a bit of information about your business. If a Google Places listing for your practice doesn't exist, you can create one yourself through your main Google account.

When optimized properly, a Google Places listing can generate a substantial amount of targeted traffic to a website because it focuses on Google users searching for specific local products and services. It also is a highly effective way to reach mobile users who may actually be just a few blocks away and searching for your practice at that particular moment.

> If you can only open one online business directory listing, it needs to be a Google Places listing.

11 more top online business directories

Although Google Places is arguably the most important business directory listing you can have, there are a number of other high SEO-value business directories that also provide free basic listings and can generate some free traffic for you. They include:

1. yp.com (Yellow Pages)
2. manta.com
3. yellowusapages.com
4. citysearch.com
5. yelp.com
6. 7mainstreet.com
7. merchantcircle.com
8. superpages.com
9. yellowbot.com
10. insiderpages.com
11. expressupdate.com

All of them require email verification when you create a directory listing for the first time, but the overall process for registering with each of them is fairly straightforward.

Citation consistency and completeness

Citations are the basic bundles of standardized information you provide to the directories about your business. Business name, mailing address, and your telephone number constitute the main required data elements of a citation. To derive maximum value from them, you need to ensure that the data is consistently entered in exactly the same way in every business listing. This helps avoid confusing the search engines about the identity of your business and also helps associate both trust and relevancy with your Google Places page.

> The more citations Google can find about your business, the more relevancy and authority it will award to your business' website.

It also boosts relevancy and visitor "stickiness" if all the information fields are populated. All the basic fields require data to be entered into them, but for full exploitation of the directory's value all of the optional fields should also be filled out. Never pass up the opportunity to add as many high-quality photos as you can – particularly both exterior and interior images of your chiropractic practice office – not only because they add more tangibility and visually compelling social proof to your listing, but also because their filenames also provide some influential keyword optimization value.

Some of the directories also allow you to post videos of your business in your directory listing. Videos can lend powerfully persuasive weight to your marketing message, and can also add extra SEO value that Google calculates for the overall search ranking of the directory entry. There will be more on the value of video marketing later in this book.

Care should be taken not to try to game the directory listings by engaging in spammy techniques like keyword stuffing in the description areas, entering keywords as the business name (unless that keyword is an actual part of it), and misusing the business categories used to classify the business type with.

Most, if not all, business directories use a human review process to screen new directory submissions for spammy entries and will quickly ban any that are deemed to be of questionable value or legitimacy. If for some reason you should suffer the loss of a Google Places listing or one of any other major business directories due to these kinds of infractions, it will be very difficult to have it reinstated.

Google is always modifying its relevancy and ranking algorithms to weed out the spammers and low value entries in order to improve their users' search experience. Sticking to legitimate data entry methods and providing searcher-valuable content is the best way to stay on the good side of the business directories who offer these free marketing services to business owners like you.

Recommendation

Yes, claim and develop your Google Places listing. Google's increasing emphasis on local search results makes it an even more critical element in your practice's marketing program. Your Places listing, working correctly in tandem with your primary website, can help you actually dominate Google's top ten page 1 rankings for your chosen keywords. The more links that appear on page 1 that lead back to your practice's website, the more new clients you should attract. Both on-page and off-page SEO optimization strategies also directly apply to your Places listing, with citation consistency playing a major role in its overall effectiveness.

Take full advantage of the many free directory listings. They will help increase your professional exposure, send even more free traffic back to your primary website, and add valuable netcentricity to your overall internet marketing program.

Fig. 5.1 – Use Google Places and other business directories

Chapter 6 - Social Proof: Reviews, Surveys & Testimonials

Online business directories also provide visitors with a way to review and rate the local companies they've done business with. Customer reviews, testimonials, feedback and rating scales are all examples of what is called "social proof" in internet marketing circles or "informational social influence" in more scientific circles.

Returning momentarily to the concept of K-L-T (know-like-trust) as it relates to gaining a prospect's trust before they'll convert into being a customer, the importance of having positive social proof for your business cannot be overstated. How you portray your practice on your websites to visitors is one thing, but written reviews and feedback offered by independent 3rd parties brings a completely different type of credibility to your business. What other people are saying publicly about your practice can heavily influence the decisions of others who are still in the research stage of decision-making. If they see that you have satisfied clients, it will help remove their fears of potential dissatisfaction later.

In addition, people generally find other peoples' opinions interesting. Reviews and testimonials attract attention and engage the viewer because people are naturally curious about other people's comments, particularly when they're discussing a product or service that they themselves are also in the market for. Most people are more inclined to put stock in a friend's or relative's compliment or complaint than to believe blatantly commercial sales copy.

> If an online searcher is presented with two review sites – one that has positive review comments in it about your business, and another *just below it* that has negative comments - 70% of the time searchers will click to read the negative reviews first.
>
> That doesn't help you make a good first impression.

You can't afford not to engage

Whether your practice is on the web or not, customers will still talk about it online, and the comments can be either commendatory or critical. People are subconsciously drawn to reading critical comments and ratings. Negative reviews may end up ranking highly in search engine results, and the more visible they are, the more they will probably have a seriously damaging effect upon someone's business.

It is next to impossible to have negative comments – justified or unjustified – removed from review sites, so a business owner's only real choice is to go ahead and engage in those forums. Most sites allow owners to respond to any comments made about their businesses, so this represents an excellent opportunity for the business owner to either try to reclaim the disgruntled customer with a sincere acknowledgment of the grievance or respectfully refute the negative review.

When other visitors see that you took the time to objectively address the cause of someone's dissatisfaction – especially when it means accepting responsibility for the things that can and do go occasionally wrong in a chiropractic practice - it paints you and your practice in a favorable light. People want to see responsibility accepted and not just excused away, and this can go a long way toward helping maintain your positive public reputation.

And here is a simple business observation from my many years of leading and optimizing service-oriented business units for some very large companies. Legitimate complaints from customers represent valuable feedback that provides you with an opportunity to further improve your business. Business owners should learn to shrug off the embarrassment and pain that criticism naturally causes for people like them who care deeply about their business, and take the steps necessary to keeping that mistake from reoccurring. Not only will they have a better product or service to sell in the long run, but they may very well keep that disgruntled customer from leaving forever since they saw that they were taken seriously.

Granted, it's not always easy to do because it forces you to take action about something, but again, long-term retention of your customers is one of the key secrets to having a profitable and sustainable business. Taking action and demonstrating your commitment to providing superior service is always worth the time and effort involved.

> Rather than simply ignoring it, it is critically important to become an active participant of the inevitable public online conversation about you.

Actively managing your own online brand

There are two primary components to an effective reputation management program for your business:

1. Implementing an "every day" in-house patient survey process and having the results posted as reviews on review sites.

2. Proactively monitoring your online reputation and immediately intervening when required.

Patient surveys

As previously mentioned, customer reviews, ratings and feedback posted on review sites are highly influential with prospects when trying to determine whether or not they'll patronize your practice. In fact, online reviews – and the all-important "5 gold star rating" – are quickly becoming more powerful influencers than even word-of-mouth marketing.

Community and Social Tools That Impact Buying	
User-generated product reviews	59%
Online customer Q&A on product sites	42%
Community forums	26%
User-generated videos	15%
Facebook company Pages	13%
Facebook newsfeeds	13%
Mobile (iPhone, apps, text messages)	9%
Twitter (monitor, respond, post tweets)	9%

Source: the etailing group / PowerReviews, June 2011

Surveying your customers regularly should be an integral part of not only your chiropractic practice's marketing program but also its daily service delivery plan. Ideally, just before a patient leaves your office after being seen, they should be politely asked to fill out a concise (yet meaningful) paper survey that your staff provides them on a clipboard with a pen. By making this face-to-face "call to action", this now becomes your best chance to capture this important social proof for use in your online marketing program. (And not only to gather social proof, but also as actionable internal feedback and as an implicit ongoing reminder to your staff that you do care about the service your office provides.)

If the patient declines but instead asks to take the survey with them and send it back later, you can count on a much lower response rate because few will be motivated enough to follow through with it. To improve your chances, be prepared to also provide them with a self-addressed stamped envelope along with your survey form if you want to make it as easy as possible for them to get that important data back to you. Emailing a reminder to them after their visit is also a possibility but, again, expect a lower response rate than what you would get from making a face-to-face request.

In either case, to simplify the process even further for them, be sure to include on the paper survey form or in your email the URL (internet address) to your Google Places listing page. This will make it easier for them to log into Google and fill out its online review form.

Additionally, there should always be an easily recognizable link on your website to an electronic version of your customer satisfaction survey. This can be a form-based web page on which the patient fills in various fields, with the results then being automatically sent in email format to an email account that you have designated for storing and managing your reviews.

To ensure HIPAA compliance, the survey should only ask questions about the quality of the patient's visit (e.g., cleanliness of the facilities, friendliness and professionalism of staff, timeliness of services rendered, parking availability, and other non-treatment issues). Respondents should also be given the option to submit their surveys anonymously if they choose to.

Google is watching

Because of the increasing importance of customer reviews to the overall search engine ranking process, Google and the other review sites are closely monitoring both the review content and **from where the reviews were submitted.**

Here are some important caveats to keep in mind when actively running a customer review program:

- Submission of fake reviews is unethical and should never be condoned. Increasingly accurate software algorithms using psychometric criteria are now being deployed by review websites to help screen out fake reviews.

- A review should be submitted to only one online review site as duplicates are discarded wherever detected.

- Google prohibits “incentivizing” patients in any way to submit reviews, as it is thought that it could influence their responses.

- If your staff is collecting paper surveys from patients, those surveys **should not** be entered into your Google Places listing by anyone working in your office. Review sites like Google Places, YP.com, and Yelp can easily track the IP address (a unique number assigned to every internet-connected device) of the submitter. If they see a number of reviews all being submitted from one IP address - or a series of closely related IPs – those reviews will almost certainly be construed as fake (whether they are or not) and be discarded.

- Should Google sense that there are dubious activities occurring with your Places site, they can remove it without warning and all the highly valuable benefits that a Places site affords will be lost.

Recommendation

Yes, by all means implement a formal in-house patient review program if you haven't already to gather written surveys from at least some of your patients every day. Working with your staff, an experienced internet marketing consultant can help design the actual survey form and take care of getting the patient surveys reviews properly posted to Google Places and other customer review sites.

Your business needs at least five written reviews to be able to show a "star" rating in Google Places, so the more reviews you can accumulate and the sooner you get them posted online, the better.

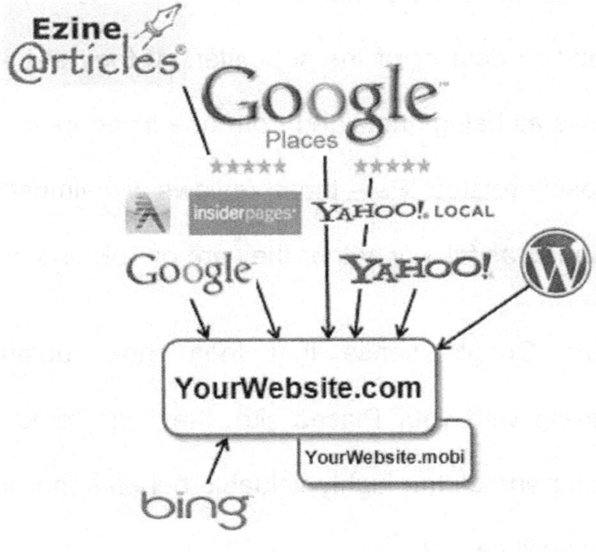

Fig. 6.1 – 5 gold star reviews are crucial in developing K-L-T

Advertising and using patient testimonials

Just as in other medical fields, the use of patient testimonials in a chiropractic practice's marketing program is an interesting and controversial issue because it continues to bring with it a number of questions about propriety and legality. Compliance with current ACA marketing guidelines might be a good place to start looking for answers, so let's take a look at what their guidance basically states:

- Be sure that any testimonial or success story that you use in your advertising represents the type of results you would *routinely* expect to see in your chiropractic office.
- Make sure that you have sufficient written documentation of the facts, as well as documentation on a number of other similar cases that, again, would serve to demonstrate this type of *typical* result.
- You can't make misleading statements or misrepresent yourself in any way, nor can your testimonial providers.

According to Texas state law, chiropractors can advertise their services as long as the advertisements are not fraudulent and don't make unverifiable claims that their performance is superior to others.

Neither can chiropractic ads mislead people into thinking they are physicians, the law says.

Ultimately, compliance is up to you, so I would suggest paying a visit to your state licensing board's website periodically to stay up to date on rules and regulations in this particular aspect of your practice. To find your state board's web site, visit the Federation of Chiropractic Licensing Boards online at www.fclb.org.

The opinions and suggestions presented here are for informational purposes only and not for the purpose of providing legal advice. You should consult your attorney or contact your state's licensing board to obtain advice with respect to marketing, promotions, or any other legal issues.

Testimonials vs reviews

Although these two types of social proof share many of the same characteristics, there are some significant differences between them:

Testimonials:	Reviews:
• are completely controlled by the business. They can choose only to publish the positive.	• exist outside of the business' control. They have little to no control over what is posted.
• are usually hosted on the business' website.	• are usually hosted on independent websites.
• are always positive, most of them overwhelmingly so.	• can be negative, positive, or even neutral.
• frequently are viewed by the reader as being just another form of advertising	• are not viewed as cynically by the reader and are seen to be more credible than testimonials

Recommendation

Testimonials are viewed more skeptically than reviews by the casual reader. **Considering the significant legal risks that may exist in using patient testimonials, customer reviews are seen here as being the preferred (and already common) method for providing effective - and potentially less problematic - social proof.**

CHAPTER 7 - Reputation Management & Recovery

Reputation management

What happens, though, when you've been unjustly or maliciously maligned online? Competition can be particularly vicious in certain business niches, and although Google and other review sites try mightily to ensure the legitimacy of their posted reviews, it's still not unheard of for business rivals to post false, negative comments online to disparage their competitors' reputations.

Along with the rise of the online review sites has emerged a new business service called online **reputation management.** It combines several key functions that, when actively managed, can help a chiropractic practice not only maintain a positive reputation online but burnish its professional image even further.

And what about a business that has no online reviews or other types of customer feedback that searchers can refer to? **Having no online reputation is almost as bad as having a negative reputation.** It does not help give the impression – *the all-important impression that would spur a potential patient to make a leap of faith and try your* *practice for the first time* – that that particular practice is regularly patronized or even formally established.

One of the first challenges, then, that newcomers to a particular business niche must overcome is how to demonstrate their professional bona fides. Earning positive customer reviews is an excellent way to start legitimizing oneself.

Reputation management, then, is all about continually building a compelling positive narrative about your business through the use of positive customer reviews. It also means actively addressing the negative feedback any business owner inevitably gets in order to mitigate the reputational damage to their business it may have caused.

Recommendation

If you already have an active, ongoing patient survey process in operation, you have taken the most important step toward having a formal reputation management program for your chiropractic practice. A comprehensive reputation management program, though, will also include regularly monitoring the internet for any other references to you or your business, including what's being said about you on the most popular social media sites. This affords you the opportunity to respond to both positive and negative commentary if you wish.

Reputation recovery

An active reputation management program that is already working effectively for you should obviate the need for what's called a reputation recovery program. **Reputation recovery** generally takes the form of an all-out, multi-faceted, tightly-orchestrated SEO campaign designed to counter negative publicity about a business on review sites and other online resources that have been given prominently high rankings on SERPs (search engine results pages, like page 1 of Google).

Imagine that you performed a Google search on your own chiropractic practice, and out of Google's ten listings on its first page many were review sites or blog posts reflecting negative comments about you. A reputation recovery program would basically take these two steps to deal with these negative listings:

First, on Google's search engine results page, it will begin to **isolate** individual negative listings with newly created positive listings of your own, surrounding the negative entries in a way that helps deflect searcher attention away from the negative information.

Secondly, it will **displace** the negative listings by pushing them further down the SERP, moving them off of page 1 to page 2, and then to page 3 where they will effectively be pushed out of view for any searcher.

Depending upon the extent of the negative information and the degree of competitiveness for the keywords that would generate a particular SERP, an effective reputation recovery program should be expected to be both relatively expensive and to take a number of months to fully implement.

> Having a proactive reputation *management* program in place is highly preferable over having to mobilize an expensive reputation *recovery* program after the damage has already been done.

CHAPTER 8 – SOCIAL MEDIA

Social media explodes

Facebook.com is perhaps the best known of the main social media websites today, and "social media" is *the* fastest growing segment of the internet by far over the last couple of years. Interactive company blogs and social sites like Facebook, Twitter and LinkedIn are among the best known examples of this booming internet phenomenon.

Social media sites like Facebook are essentially online communities where people can come together to exchange information, share messages and pictures, have discussions, form like-minded interest groups, and otherwise engage with each other using a common technology platform that is easy and free to use. These sites can be accessed on both desktop computers and, increasingly, mobile devices.

- In 2011, 61% of all US citizens who spent time online spent it using social networking sites.
- 35% of them spent over 3 hours online every day.

Source: "Digital Marketing Budget Trends for 2012", 6smarketing.com, October 2011

In its filing for an IPO expected later this year, Facebook stated that it has 845 million users worldwide, up 39% over last year. Twitter's numbers are thought to be in the 125 million user range. Those extremely large concentrations of people represent large attractive pools of prospective customers that many companies would very much like to market to.

Social Media Sites That Have Generated Customers For Companies

Company blogs ---------------------------------- 57%

LinkedIn -- 57%

Twitter ------------------------------------ 48%

Facebook ------------------------ 42%

Source: "Digital Marketing Budget Trends for 2012", 6smarketing.com, October 2011

In fact, it's estimated that about 1 million US companies have already established their own corporate presences on Facebook, and many more are rushing now to stake out their own free pages.

Facebook is free but now monetized

Facebook's stated mission is "to give people the power to share and make the world more open and connected." To do that, it maintains two different personas: its primary reason for being, the social side, and its now-emerging commercial side – and it works diligently to keep them separate yet available to each other.

The original intent behind Facebook was to give college friends a way to keep in touch after leaving school. It quickly grew into a world-wide application designed to facilitate social interaction and communication. Facebook wants its user community to have fun and spend time on the site without being besieged on all sides by advertising. Blatantly commercial activity was not only frowned upon but actively punished. Facebook users themselves were also involved participants, self-policing its community and keeping the encroachment of crass commercialization at bay.

As hundreds of millions of people set up personal **Profile Pages** on Facebook, though, it became increasingly costly to continue offering these services for free. As a result, Facebook implemented an internal advertising platform called **Facebook Ads** where advertisers could bid on rotating ad space in much the same fashion as Google did with Adwords.

This huge following of users is allowing Facebook to build one of the largest demographic / sociographic databases in the world. A Facebook user is encouraged to describe herself in her online profile in the minutest amount of detail, from where she lives and how old she is, all the way down to the fact that she's an Elvis fan and drives a blue Corvette convertible to work every week, for example. This is an amazingly powerful opportunity for advertisers since Facebook's data can be mined, analyzed and used in highly targeted ad campaigns.

As of this writing, Facebook is moving millions of dollars through its bids-based Ads platform daily, with new features and applications being introduced regularly as it continues to evolve through these early stages. Many businesses are also seeing additional profits driven by Facebook Ads contribute directly to their own bottom lines.

> Having a Facebook page has become required for any company of any size because Facebook users have now come to expect it.

Facebook requires a more subtle touch

The other method in which Facebook allows commercial activity to occur on its site is through the use of **Facebook Pages**. As opposed to the personal profile that individuals create for themselves, Pages are public profiles enabling a business to share its products and services with Facebook users. The "viral" marketing aspect of it occurs when "fans" "like" your Page and stories linking back to it are shared with their friends – and then get shared again and again - via their personal News Feeds.

Because of the predominantly strong social overtones to Facebook, however, experienced marketers find that a more circumspect approach to advertising using Facebook Pages is the most effective way to market to its user base. Instead of the obviously commercial, in-your-face type of selling that we commonly see used in other types of marketing channels (and for which may be perfectly apropos), savvy Facebook marketers understand that Facebook users, above all, need to be given the chance to gradually warm up to any commercial pitches they're thrown before they'll respond.

And again, as with any other type of online marketing tool you choose to use, that ever-present KLT (know-like-trust) factor reigns supreme here too. Establishing professional legitimacy, giving something of value to them, and earning their trust is the first key to getting people to choose to do business with you.

> About 20% of all social media patrons use it to glean medical-related information from.
>
> **Source:** April 2011 survey by the National Research Corporation

For example, you should first make an effort to earn your Facebook visitors' trust by regularly (at least once daily) posting chiropractic-related information on your Page's Timeline that you think they'll find interesting and useful. Offering self-help tips, links to relevant chiropractic news stories or videos, and seasonal reminders about chiropractic issues are all good candidates that can help demonstrate your authority. Asking questions and taking simple polls are also great ways to stimulate interaction, help strike up the conversation, and begin some dialogue online with your customers.

Engage on Facebook, but draw the line...

Social media makes interaction between patients and chiropractors easier than ever, but chiropractors still need to be wary of crossing the privacy line. Providing general information and responding to generic chiropractic questions using social media is perfectly appropriate and much appreciated by your audience, but when a discussion begins to veer into personal chiropractic questions, the conversation either needs to be re-routed to a suggestion for scheduling a formal office visit, or simply remove the discussion thread from the social media site.

Before building a social media presence online, you should develop written policies and procedures to help guide those on your staff and any 3rd-party service providers who will interact in this forum. In fact, it would be wise to incorporate your social media policy within your overall HIPAA compliance program, and make sure your employees understand what is permissible online and what is not.

Engaging on Facebook can also put an additional squeeze on chiropractors' already-full schedules, but the time it takes to make an occasional post online can be well worth it simply because of all the good will it generates. People are generally aware of the constraints chiropractors have on them, and a simple expression of caring by taking a minute to answer a visitor's question can go a long way to overcoming that formidable KLT barrier. Your staff can be trained to answer simple administrative questions or make the generic informational posts daily, and can notify you when a more specific chiropractic question needs a response.

Recommendation

Yes, by all means set up a Facebook Page for your practice. An interactive, regularly-updated Facebook Page can be a valuable online asset in many ways for any chiropractic practice. Talk to your internet marketing consultant about setting one up with custom graphics and features for your own business. If you or your staff don't have the capacity to manage the daily activity on it, most consultants will also handle the daily "care and feeding" of your Facebook Page by making regular posts of relevant content to it and informing you or your office staff of any specific chiropractic questions being asked online that require your professional attention.

Facebook Ads may also be an appropriate advertising vehicle for you to use to drive traffic to your website as its highly detailed user demographics allow you to target specific types of prospects in specific geographical locations. A chiropractor who treats sports injuries may, for example, run ads targeting sports clubs or leagues in your local area. Ask your marketing consultant to do some preliminary keyword research to help you determine what kind of advertising strategy and budget may be appropriate for a Facebook Ads campaign.

Twitter - to tweet or not to tweet?

Twitter.com, another hugely popular social media site, allows its users to communicate via smartphone or computer using 140-character messages, or “Tweets”, sent to other people who opt to “follow” them. Also a free service, Twitter is effective in getting short messages distributed quickly to a large number of people simultaneously. Twitter is also ideal for use on mobile devices where being able to quickly and easily send brief messages to your list of followers is important.

Some chiropractic professionals are leveraging the real-time aspects of social media to help improve their services and show more sensitivity to their patients’ own challenges and concerns. Chiropractors are starting to use Twitter as a way to alert patients when they’re running late for appointments that day, thereby helping their patients reduce the amount of time they would otherwise spend unnecessarily in the chiropractor's waiting room.

Other chiropractors use Twitter to remind their patients of events like National Chiropractic Day (September 16), National Bone and Joint Health Awareness Week (October 12-20), and other health-related events that occur only infrequently. These are also the types of events that Twitter users feel comfortable tweeting their own friends and followers about, further spreading your professional image in a positive and useful way.

Just as in the case of Facebook and other social media channels, chiropractors need to ensure they're drawing the correct boundaries around patient privacy issues and staying true to them. The good news is that more clear guidance continues to emerge over time.

Recommendation

Yes, you can use Twitter in a limited manner for your chiropractic practice, but I would suggest only after you have fully implemented a higher-value Facebook Page (it has six times as many users as Twitter) and gotten comfortable with the type and pace of personal interaction that takes place in that venue. Once you establish an online social media presence in a certain channel, your fans and followers will expect to see regular engagement on your part take place there. If you neglect it, their attraction to it will dwindle and you'll most assuredly lose their attention.

Social media has never been more important to a business than it is today because that's where the new generation of customers are – better informed, frequently online, and looking for providers of products and services who agree to meet them using the communication channels of *their* choice.

LinkedIn – social media for professionals

The third major player in the social media arena is **LinkedIn.com**. A relative newcomer to the social media game, LinkedIn's claim to fame is being the world's largest social media site designed for business professionals with over 150 million registered users.

> It's estimated that LinkedIn is currently growing at a rate faster than two new members per second.

LinkedIn's business-to-business (B2B) orientation is the major difference between it and the other social media sites, but if we look closely, there are a number of similar features it shares with Facebook.

Each site expects you to define yourself initially via a profile page (Facebook is more of a personal profile, while LinkedIn asks for your professional qualifications). In addition to your profiles, each site allows you to create another resource (Facebook's Page and LinkedIn's Company page) that describes your business entity.

In LinkedIn, you can network with other professionals either one-on-one or more publicly through participation in its various "Groups" of like-minded people which are centered around a specific business topic. LinkedIn Groups also offer their members the convenience of sending out daily and weekly digests of their happenings to help them stay current with the conversations taking place in those forums.

Basic LinkedIn membership is free. LinkedIn also has its own onboard PPC advertising program called LinkedIn Ads, similar to both Google's AdWords and Facebook's Ads systems. Your ads are displayed on prominent LinkedIn pages, and you can target your audience by job type, industry, geography, gender, age, or LinkedIn group.

Recommendation

Yes, join LinkedIn but for purely peer-to-peer professional networking purposes. This isn't the right environment to prospect for additional consumer clients. Much in the same way you may have joined chiropractic associations to help you keep abreast of changes in your industry and to establish professional relationships within your field, LinkedIn Groups provides you with the same "birds of a feather" environment for professional networking. It can also make it easier for you to identify joint venture or partnership opportunities either within your chosen niche or across related business verticals.

LinkedIn also has its own PPC advertising program similar in many ways to Google's and Facebook's, but again, it's more business-to-business focused. Unless you envision wanting to actively solicit for potential joint venture partners via paid advertising, for example, LinkedIn's advertising program may not be something you'd need to engage in early on.

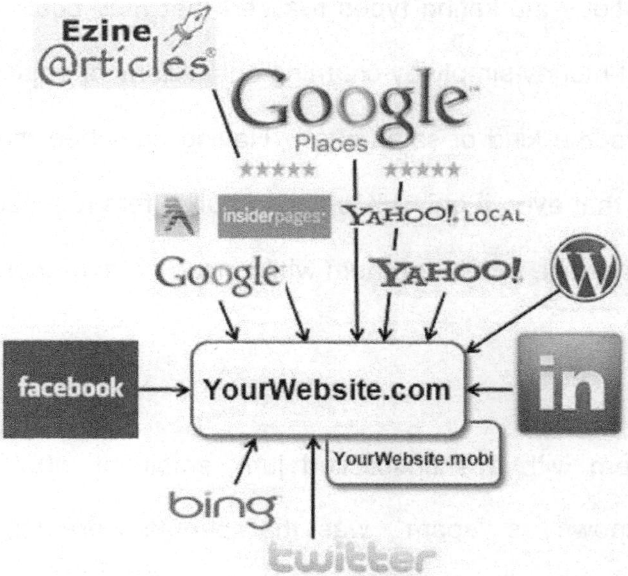

FIG. 8.1 – YOUR SOCIAL MEDIA SITES DRIVE TRAFFIC TO YOUR WEBSITE

CHAPTER 9 – Email Marketing

Email marketing has come a long way since the early days of the internet. Back in the early 1990s when the internet's presence was first being felt in a major way, email was one of the first internet applications that people gravitated heavily toward. A cheap, easy and efficient way to communicate, email quickly became a communication staple for many people both at work and at home. However, because email was also completely unregulated at the time, ambitious marketing types realized that they could make vast amounts of money simply by churning out millions of emails daily that contained some kind of sales offer. Having crunched the numbers, they knew that even if only 1% of those bulk offers resulted in a sale, it still meant huge profits for them while incurring extremely low costs in the process.

The problem with this unsolicited junk email, or what commonly became known as "spam", was that people were literally being bombarded with the stuff on a daily basis, cluttering up their inboxes and wreaking havoc with corporate email systems, networks, and internet service providers.

As a result, federal legislation called the "CAN-SPAM Act" was passed in 2003. It set forth the rules for commercial email by giving individuals the right not to receive them and also spelled out tough penalties for violators. These rules cover all commercial messages, not just bulk email.

Email marketing is 1-to-1 relationship marketing

Fast forwarding to today (and after a number of subsequent highly publicized spammer convictions under the new spam laws), the email environment has become relatively tamer since those wilder early days. What's interesting, though, is that the same dynamic – that a certain percentage of people **will** respond favorably to email sales promotions – still exists today, and that has lead to the next generation of email marketing called "permission-based" marketing.

"Permission-based" marketing, also known as "opt in" marketing, works because instead of sending unsolicited emails to people who have no interest in the offer being made, emails are instead sent routinely to people who **are** interested in receiving them. They have already performed some action like filling out a short form and supplying their email address to demonstrate their willingness to receive future emails. Their permission is usually granted in exchange for receiving something of value to them like a free report, newsletter subscription, or some other instantly deliverable information product.

Seth Godin, one of the internet's early and most visionary marketing pioneers, stated his view of permission marketing this way:

"The first rule of permission marketing is that it's based on selfishness. Consumers will grant a company permission to communicate (with them) only if they know what's in it for them...Permission marketing turns strangers into friends and friends into loyal customers. It's not just about entertainment - it's about education."

- 95% of internet users have given permission to a company to send them information through email.
- 72% of study participants preferred email for receiving promotional messages from companies with which they had granted permission to send them ongoing information.
- 65% of internet users have made a purchase as a result of a marketing message they received through email.

Source: ExacTarget 2008 Channel Preference Survey

Implementing email marketing in your practice

The best place to capture your website visitors' email addresses is on your website using a brief "opt-in" form. **This form should be visible in the top half of every page of your website.** Visitors enter their name and email address into the form, and when they submit it, you can have it set up so that their free information product is automatically emailed back to them using an email management tool called an autoresponder. At the same time, they'll also be added to an email list containing all of the other "opt in" subscribers you've gathered. As your list grows, so does your potential patient base.

It wouldn't be unheard of to accumulate hundreds or thousands of contacts on your email list over time. Experienced marketers commonly divide larger lists into sub-lists, each perhaps being a slightly different target market and needing to receive a different type of communication.

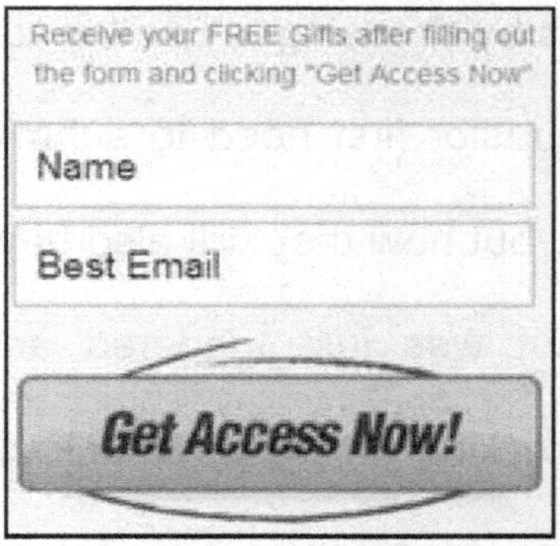

The all-important "opt in" form

Requiring that your prospects opt in (i.e., provide you with their information) gives you the permission you need to enter into a legitimate marketing relationship with your website visitors (that is, with potential patients).

This is called the “single opt in” method because it only requires one action on the requestor’s part – submitting their name and email address. Although this requirement has significantly reduced the number of spam complaints coming from consumers, people do occasionally forget that they previously “opted in” and then file spam complaints anyway when they receive the next email.

To further reduce the risk of spam complaints, businesses frequently safeguard themselves by choosing to use the “double opt in” method. Not only will the requestor first need to submit their email address using the opt in form, but now they will also have to actively respond to another email that was just triggered and sent to them via autoresponder. By clicking on a certain link in that email, they will have effectively opted in twice, which takes a more significant conscious effort. Forcing that second opt-in action virtually eliminates the chance of future spam complaints.

Your list of email addresses will become one of the most valuable information assets in your business. It’s your list of current and prospective clients. And as they say in internet marketing:

"The money is in the list."

Your email opt-in list represents a group of "warm" prospects that are now aware of your existence by virtue of having visited your website. You can now send them a series of coordinated follow-up email messages automatically at certain intervals using a series of autoresponders. If you use this strategy to share free, high value content with them regularly, you will have begun the process of letting them get to know you, like you, and trust you enough to want to become your patient.

Some of the various types of chiropractic content that many patients find valuable today and would voluntarily opt-in to receiving include:

- Bi-weekly or monthly newsletters identifying chiropractic trends, including self-help tips on how to maintain good spinal health, information on topics such as head and neck pain, stress management, children's health, new chiropractic techniques now in use, or any number of chiropractic-related topics;

- Notices of new clinical studies and information on how patients can participate in them;
- Reminders of recurring events such as chiropractic adjustments, and ongoing self-care reminders (i.e, diet, sleep, exercise, etc.);
- Coupons for discounts on various services you offer, particularly those intended to attract new patients.

To be in compliance with the CAN-SPAM act, every email sent to your list must contain your full business address and a link for them to “opt out” of receiving future correspondence at any time.

Recommendation

Yes, incorporate email marketing into your overall internet marketing program. Email marketing today is an effective and inexpensive way to not only attract new prospective patients to your chiropractic practice but also strengthen your relationships with the patients you already have.

Just as with any meaningful relationship, it takes some effort to maintain and, ideally, improve it. Current and prospective clients will usually appreciate your efforts to provide additional value to them with nothing expected in return. This keeps you "top of mind" when it is time to schedule a chiropractic appointment with someone.

If you can provide your internet marketing consultant with some high value content that you think would be of interest your audience, your consultant will be able to take that content and set up everything you need to implement an effective email marketing system for your practice. Or tell your consultant what topics you'd like to cover and they'll do the research for you. The longer your autoresponder sequences can run delivering fresh content – ideally for months at a time - the more effective your email marketing program can be.

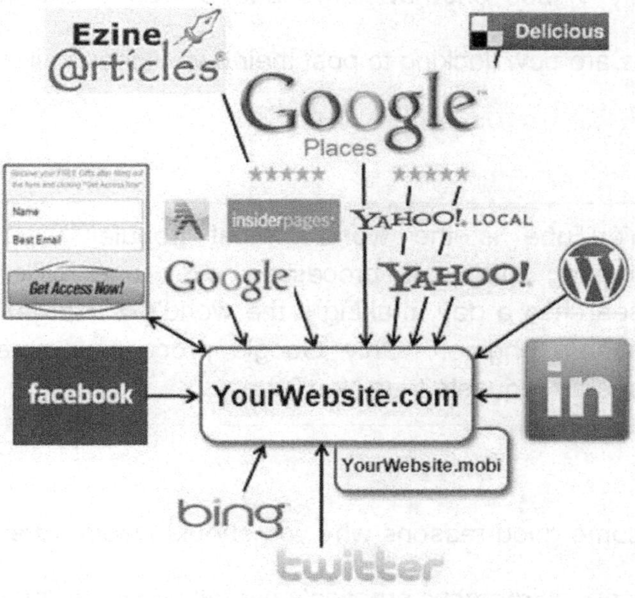

Fig. 9.1 – Have your email opt-in form visible on every webpage

CHAPTER 10 – VIDEO MARKETING

Video marketing is yet another highly effective way to market your chiropractic practice online, and many chiropractors are already using video today to their public relations advantage. Video is one of the most powerful types of media in use because of the richer sensory spectrum through which it allows communication to occur.

If you haven't heard of **YouTube.com**, you should make it a point to spend some time there. It's one of the most highly trafficked websites on the internet today, and its use has grown far beyond hosting silly videos shot at home and posted online for laughs. Businesses are now flocking to post their own videos to it.

> YouTube is the world's most popular video sharing site. It processes over one billion searches a day, making it the world's 2nd largest search engine. Only Google processes more search requests than YouTube.

Here are some good reasons why you should incorporate the use of video into your chiropractic practice's overall marketing program:

- It's a highly effective way to let prospects see who you are, kicking off that all-important know-like-trust process which inevitably leads to some conversions to patients;

- Video can clearly convey your chiropractic authority and professional qualifications by allowing visitors to see and hear you in your work environment (but not necessarily working);

- You can visually introduce prospects to your practice's office location, your staff members, your office's intake procedures, and anything else you'd like to "pull the curtains back" on to increase visitors' familiarity with you and your practice;

- Video is a natural medium for learning (many people learn better from watching video than reading printed materials), and educational videos are another excellent way to demonstrate your credentials while providing useful, valuable information to your visitors.

Recommendation

Yes, include video marketing throughout your overall online marketing program. The more quality video content you can include in your online marketing materials, the easier it will be to attract viewers and ultimately turn some of them into paying customers. People respond well to the video medium and its importance in your overall online marketing plan simply cannot be overstated.

Keeping it real

Not all that long ago, having commercial videos created for marketing purposes cost quite a bit of money and took what seemed to be an inordinate amount of time to produce. That isn't the case anymore. Videos can be shot, produced, and published very quickly and inexpensively now. They can follow a variety of formats, but the most popular types of videos are produced around:

- an interview with the chiropractor, and perhaps also the office manager;
- a walking tour of your practice, ideally getting a smile and a wave from each of your staff members along the way;
- a quick tour of your practice and a brief self-introduction by each staffer;
- the chiropractor speaking about a particular chiropractic problem, and the appropriate treatment method for it;

- the office manager demonstrating the new patient intake process or another type of administrative procedure.

These videos don't have to be any longer than two or three minutes in length and can be easily filmed in your office in a brief visit by your videographer or marketing consultant.

> Studies have shown that simple, short duration, reality-style videos are more effective in conveying personality and earning trust than slick-looking, obviously commercially produced videos.

Getting your videos online

The proliferation of high-speed internet access and vast amounts of cheap storage has hastened the spread of video throughout everything online; it's just easier and more cost-effective to do now. Video can and should be added to just about any online asset you own or have the ability to add it to, including:

- Your website or blog, particularly its homepage;

- Your Google Places business listing (you can add up to five videos);
- Your Facebook and LinkedIn Pages;
- Any other business directory listings you have.

It's also easy to embed clickable links to your videos in any kind of electronic correspondence such as newsletters, emails, tweets, and Facebook posts. People who enjoy your videos will share them with other people, increasing their viral spread and introducing even more prospects to you and your chiropractic practice.

Additional video benefits

Since video is important to Google's goal of being able to provide the best possible search experience to its customers, it shouldn't be surprising to learn that – despite having their own video sharing service called Google Video - Google also bought YouTube several years ago.

This has, arguably, imbued YouTube videos with some fairly powerful SEO benefits by virtue of its close relationship with Google. It's not uncommon to see a video rank more highly on a Google SERP than the web page that was hosting the video. Testing also suggests that videos seem to get indexed by Google a little more quickly than your typical website does.

Take advantage of your own YouTube channel

Any business like yours can create its own YouTube "channel" simply by choosing to in the "Settings" area of your Google account. Once the channel has been created, you can customize it with your own graphics, colors, logos, and any other thematic properties you like.

You can also provide valuable information about your chiropractic practice in your YouTube profile, including a link back to your primary website. This link conveys high SEO value to your site, so it's important that this connection be made to help elevate your website's search engine rankings even more. The Description field of your YouTube channel should also be populated with a URL link back to your website and relevant keywords about your business in order to help searchers find your particular channel.

Uploading video files to your YouTube channel is also fairly straightforward. You'll want to be sure to use relevant keywords about your practice when titling and tagging your videos as this will help searchers find them using YouTube's search engine.

In fact, adding videos to your channel doesn't really have to be any more difficult than shooting a brief video clip on your iPhone or other mobile device every so often and uploading it directly to YouTube. Just as regularly adding new content to your website and other web properties is important to your visitors (and Google) from both a relevancy and freshness standpoint, adding new videos to your YouTube channel on a regular basis will also help visitors stay engaged with you **and** give your channel a boost in the authority and relevancy calculations.

When someone clicks on your video it will play for them; they will also see a link that will take them to your YouTube channel where they can see the rest of the videos you have listed. They can also read what you've written there about your practice and other peoples' comments about your videos.

The more people who like your videos by clicking on the "Like" button, the more popular they become and the more they'll be rewarded by the search engines with higher rankings. And whenever visitors "subscribe" to your YouTube channel, they'll be notified every time you post a new video to it.

Syndication to other video sharing sites

YouTube is the largest and best known video sharing site on the internet, but there are quite a few other video sites that your videos should also be posted to. This is yet another excellent way to get maximum exposure for your video content, in addition to the powerful link "juice" that flows back from those sites to your primary website.

Some of the better known and higher ranking video syndication sites where your videos should also be posted include:

Google Video	BrightCove	Photobucket	Viddler
Metacafe	Pandora	DailyMotion	Vimeo

Links = relevancy = traffic = patients

It's important to take a moment here and remind ourselves that each and every element described so far – every video file, web page, directory listing, image file, social media account and domain name – can be used as a unique and powerful piece of the optimization puzzle that will directly or indirectly influence the effectiveness and profitability of your online marketing program.

The more these elements can be leveraged in concert with each other to generate their optimum linking value, and the more netcentricity that you can continue to weave throughout your business, the more visibility, traffic, and ultimately profits you can realistically expect to achieve.

This is not an opportunity to just "throw some stuff against the wall and see what sticks", but instead calls for a thoughtful, carefully orchestrated marketing plan designed to meet your own unique business objectives.

Have your internet marketing consultant provide you with a written roadmap and implementation timeline showing how the various components will work together to generate high SERP rankings – and traffic - for your website, videos, and other online assets.

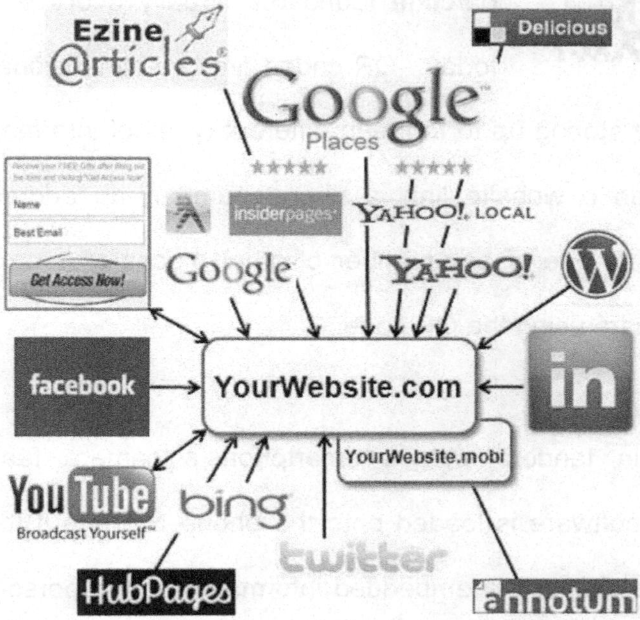

Fig. 10.1 – Allow prospects to get to know you better by having your own YouTube video channel

CHAPTER 11 – QR codes

What is a QR code?

Quick response codes, or QR codes, are essentially just another version of the ubiquitous barcode found on virtually every product sold today. QR codes are two-dimensional graphics capable of storing up to fourteen different types of information which can include a website link, a phone number, an address, a text message, or one of any number of other pieces of information you want to share using the QR code.

Working in tandem with a smartphone's camera feature, free scanning software is loaded onto the phone allowing it to scan QR codes and deliver the embedded information to the person's phone. For example, if the QR code has a link to a website in it, when the code is scanned the user will be taken automatically to that website on that phone's browser. (Remember, though, that QR codes are intended primarily for usage on mobile devices, so whatever a QR code's ultimate destination is, it needs to be optimized for easy viewing on the device's smaller display.)

QR codes can be printed on business cards, brochures, media advertisements, websites and social media pages, and anywhere else you may want to engage with your patients. Some practical uses of QR codes for a chiropractic care provider include linking to:

- patient education resources such as treatment program information, self-help tips, and dietary program outlines;
- personal introduction videos that allow prospective patients to “meet” chiropractors and initiate the trust-forming process before actually becoming patients;
- tours of your chiropractic facility;
- automated document downloads via autoresponder;
- a page where patients can tentatively schedule appointments with the chiropractor.

Recommendation

Yes, use QR codes but only as an additional mechanism to provide access to general information that should also be available through other means. Although the decades-old use of commercial barcodes is quite familiar to everyone, the recent adoption of QR code technology on a mass consumer scale has only recently begun and isn't yet widely propagated.

Patients and prospects that fall within the 22 – 37 years old demographic group are the most likely consumer segment to possess both the scanner software-equipped smartphone / tablet and the inclination to use it. Begin implementing it now within your practice to cater to both the younger and future segments of your customer base, particularly as smartphone usage increases and the application of QR code technology becomes increasingly commonplace.

Using QR codes is also a very effective way to integrate your offline marketing campaigns (direct mail, print and Yellow Pages ad, etc.) with your online marketing program, so look for opportunities to employ this kind of cross-medium linkage wherever it makes sense.

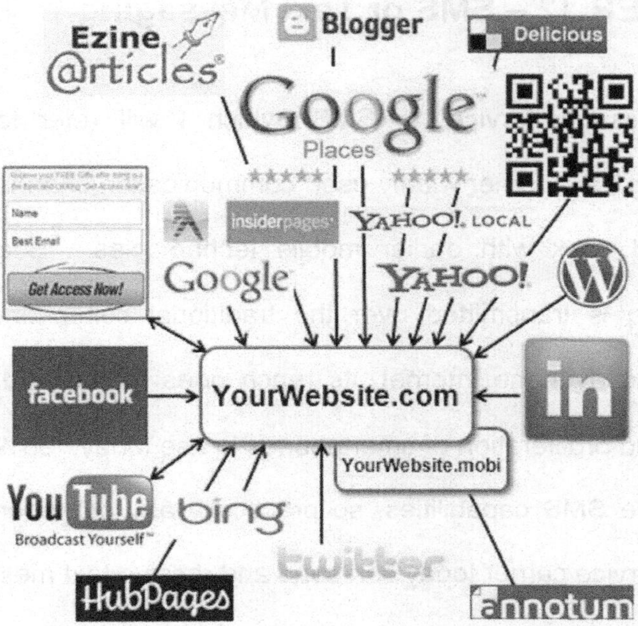

Fig. 11.1 – QR codes can direct visitors or deliver information to them

CHAPTER 12 – SMS or Text Messaging

Short message service, or SMS (which I will refer to as "text messaging") is another widely used communication channel that was introduced back with earlier mobile technologies. Because text messaging is transmitted over the traditional cell phone network rather than over the internet, its reach goes far beyond even the widespread proliferation of smartphones in use today. 96% of mobile users have SMS capabilities, so practically any cell phone on any cellular service carrier today can send and receive text messages.

A text message can contain up to 160 alphanumeric characters and is usually received immediately after being sent. It's an easy and highly effective way to quickly communicate small bites of information to either one person at a time, or to hundreds simultaneously. Just as with email addresses, SMS distribution lists can be used for mass broadcasts of information to all of the recipients on the list or can be broken down into sub-lists, each with a different purpose or audience.

In addition to its common usage, there are another couple of interesting characteristics that make text messaging attractive to marketers. SMS "open" rates (i.e., what percentage of people actually opened the message to read it instead of just deleting it) are still incredibly high, with some studies measuring open rates as high as 97%.

And not only does text messaging have a typically high open rate, but, on average, over 90% of text messages are opened *within the first four minutes* of being received.

When you compare this with the 20% average open rate for unsolicited email (and which can take days to be opened, if at all), you can clearly see how text messaging – in certain applications – can be preferable over other types of communications.

K-L-T again in play

As we've seen, getting visitors to your website to opt into an email list (for email marketing) can be a fairly easy thing to do. Offer them something free and valuable to them in exchange for their email address, and then maintain and nurture that budding relationship going forward with a continued light-handed sharing of information they'll find interesting.

However, how do you get someone to also share their cell phone number? People are generally more reluctant to share their phone number with someone because they view it as being more personal and valuable than an email address, so naturally they'll be more cautious about whom they'll entrust it to.

Again, we arrive back at the issue of K-L-T, with the establishment of Trust being the ultimate goal. Trust, as it relates to SMS marketing, is both one of its most significant advantages – and biggest challenges to overcome.

Obtaining cell phone numbers essentially depends upon the relationship you have (or don't yet have) with the people you're targeting, and the reason for which you're asking for it. Marketing products or services using text messaging isn't very effective when you don't have a relationship yet with a prospective customer and who is unfamiliar with you and your offerings. But when used with someone who already is a patient or has an existing relationship with you, it can be extremely effective.

Different acquisition methods

So just how **do** you convince your patients to give you their cell telephone numbers – and allow you to use them occasionally on an ongoing basis?

Well, before you have established the trust factor with someone, there are essentially two different methods you can use to acquire their cell phone number:

Implicit acquisition entails asking for someone's cell phone number for practical reasons like being able to send them appointment reminders and other types of time-sensitive information. Patients generally find these kinds of requests reasonable and view the text notifications themselves to be useful and appropriate when used for those types of reasons.

The best time to ask is during the new patient intake process when they're already providing you with all the other information you need to establish them as patients. An additional field on your intake form for capturing the patient's cell phone number would suffice.

With that said, though, if you also intend to use text messaging for more overt types of marketing purposes, it's important that your patients understand that and that you get their written permission. You may want to consider adding a statement making that disclosure on your HIPAA information privacy form. Another method would be add another short form to your new patient enrollment package stating that you will be using their phone number (and/or email address) periodically to send them relevant, chiropractic-related information.

As with email marketing, you also need to be sure you offer them a way to opt-out of future text notifications whenever they wish. With email, it's easy to add a few descriptive lines and the opt-out links at the bottom of the form. It's not quite that simple with text messaging, as the 160-character limit comes into play. Make sure your SMS messaging platform either accommodates higher character counts or splits overly-long messages into multiple messages to allow for the additional opt-out links and other information. Using MMS (Multimedia Messaging Service) would also circumvent the 160-character limit.

The second method for obtaining cell phone numbers is through explicit acquisition. **Explicit acquisition** means asking for peoples' cell phone numbers specifically for sending them offers and other types of marketing communications. Making requests using this upfront approach isn't quite as successful as the implicit acquisition method, but it does take the issue of permission immediately off the table.

For example, adding an optional Cell Phone field to the email opt-in form on your website would be one way to try to capture it explicitly.

How SMS marketing works

Although the traditional type of SMS marketing campaign, in my opinion, wouldn't be an appropriate candidate for a chiropractic practice to engage in (there are better methods available), I'll provide a brief overview of how SMS works in case you might think differently.

1. As a business owner, you would contract with an SMS service to provide the necessary infrastructure to send text messages to your customers. Most providers will give you a web-interfaced control panel to log into and from which you send your text messages.

2. Your SMS service provider will ask you to choose a unique “mobile keyword” that identifies your business or text messaging campaign.

3. You also choose which one of their CSCs (“common short codes”) to use; you can think of a CSC as a kind of shortened telephone number. Providers may offer you the choice of different CSCs for different levels of paid service.

4. Anyone who then texts your keyword to the CSC that you were assigned would receive an immediate text response with a message that you can customize.

5. At the same time, the customer’s cell phone number is automatically stored in your contact database. You can then

send text messages to them whenever you wish for future marketing campaigns.

So, in the case of mobile marketing campaigns, you would get your prospective customers to opt-in by running an advertisement or notice saying something like "Text the word "DoctorJones" to 45678 for free information". They would then immediately receive your pre-existing text message response and also be added automatically to your contact database.

Some SMS service providers also provide an online sign up form, or web page, so that visitors can enter their own contact information and automatically populate your contact database themselves. This is another form of the explicit acquisition method.

Recommendation

Yes, use text messaging but I would suggest that you incorporate its use into the daily patient support workflow for your chiropractic practice rather than using it for overt marketing purposes. Instead, use it as a value-added service that you provide any patients who opt to use it, providing them with automated appointment reminders.

Just using text messaging to remind patients of their next-day appointments can more than pay for itself in reducing the frequency of costly patient no-shows. It works even more effectively if your SMS service allows the recipient of the reminder to acknowledge, back through SMS, their receipt of your text message.

Taking it beyond just the concept of no-show reduction is to use SMS messaging as an “appointment recovery” system. Patients who are already in your SMS database and who have put themselves on a “short notice” list can easily and quickly be notified of any last minute cancellations by your office staff. The first patient to respond can then fill that recently-vacated appointment slot on your calendar.

Using SMS messaging to reduce the number of no-shows, along with leveraging it to quickly fill appointments cancelled at the last minute, will have an immediate positive impact on your practice’s profitability.

The practical uses of SMS messaging would provide you with even more ways to differentiate your chiropractic practice both operationally and quality of service-wise from your competitors’ practices.

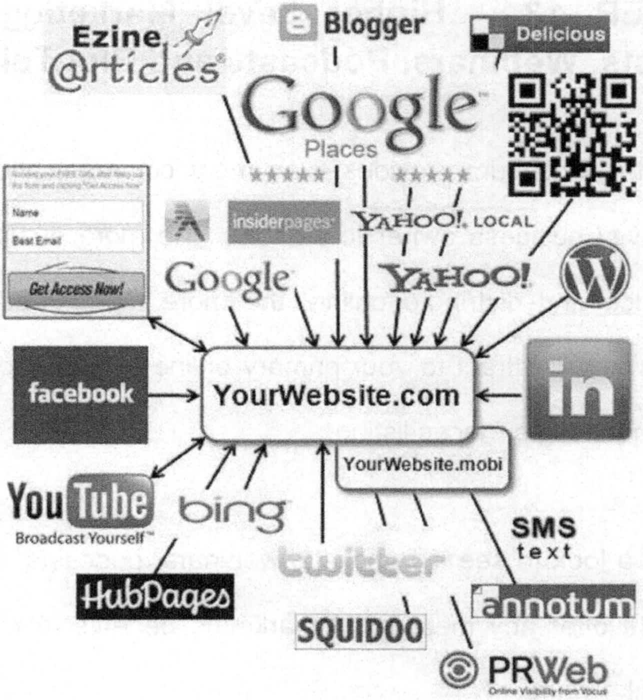

Fig. 12.1 – SMS services provide another way to provide enhanced patient support and increase practice profitability

CHAPTER 13 – Higher Level Marketing using Webcasts, Webinars, Podcasts and BlogTalkRadio

The internet continuum provides even more communication options for the savvy business owner to exploit. The more quality content you produce and distribute online, the more traffic (and potential customers) it will attract to your primary online assets such as your website and Google Places listing.

Let's take a look to see if webcasts, webinars, podcasts, or internet radio might offer any meaningful marketing benefits to chiropractic practices like yours.

What is a Webcast?

A **webcast** is an interactive live transmission of audio and/or video over the internet using so-called streaming technology. Because of the widespread proliferation of high-speed data networks and the ever-increasing penetration of the internet into today's homes and offices, webcasts can now be accessed virtually anytime, anyplace. Practically all of the major cable and broadcast networks now offer webcast services as an online adjunct to their primary transmission channels.

There are essentially two different types of webcasts. During a "live" webcast, data is streamed to the webcast participants in real time. This approach works well for any event that viewers want to watch while it happens, those typically being news and sporting events. In the other case of "on demand" webcasts, the event is recorded and stored on a remote server. Viewers can then choose where and when they wish to have the programming streamed to them.

Different types of webcasts use different types of technologies for viewing the content. Some content is delivered via internet browser like Internet Explorer, Firefox, or Chrome; other webcasts may require the installation of 3rd party software that installs on your desktop PC or mobile device and is needed to participate in the webcast.

What is a webinar?

Web-based seminars, or **webinars**, are now being offered by many companies as an effective and inexpensive alternative to holding traditional in-person seminars. Webinars, also known as online workshops, actively invite participation and offer training to its participants during hours convenient for them and that they can attend from the comfort and security of their own homes.

Webinars frequently take the form of a multi-week course, each week covering a different module or topic of study. Lecture materials, videos, and other content are uploaded regularly to the site where it can be accessed by the participants whenever they wish prior to each live webinar session. The material can remain available for review indefinitely, a big advantage over hosting in-person seminars.

The webinar speaker not only presents the material but also takes part in the discussion groups. “Typed” discussion boards are used in lieu of having face-to-face conversations. The running logs from each group can be reviewed easily by anyone anytime and provide a functional transcription of each session.

Internet-based webinars can significantly extend the reach of training programs to larger audiences while doing so in an increasingly cost effective manner. As networks continue to be upgraded to provide faster high speed online access for both consumers and businesses, look for the increased usage of live video streaming via “webcam” as an (cost) effective way to improve the quality of communication.

Recommendation

Your choice. There may be a couple of other media options available that you might prefer, so keep reading. Your choice will probably end up depending on a number of factors, namely, the type(s) of content you're willing to share, the audience(s) that content would be the most appropriate for, and the amount of time you would be able to devote to it.

Vendors

Some of the leading web conferencing systems and software include:

Citrix Online (GoToWebinar) – support for small to midsize businesses; usable on any internet-connected PC and doesn't require any software installation; webinars can be recorded for later on-demand viewing.

ReadyTalk (Web Meeting) – supports small and medium sized businesses; Flash-based player but non-Flash participants can participate via Java; supports Internet Explorer, Safari, Chrome and Firefox browsers.

Adobe (Adobe Connect Meeting) – Uses Flash platform; is accessible via web browser with the Adobe Flash Player runtime; monthly or per-use plans.

Cisco (WebEx) – support small to medium sized businesses; is provided as a service through your existing web browser; subscription-based.

iLinc (iLinc for Webinars) – another hosted service that can be used from any internet-connected PC or Macintosh; easy to facilitate small group meetings; users can share their screen, desktop, or applications

Infinite (Conferencing) – can support up to 1000 participants; focuses on small to medium sized businesses; audio or web conferencing services; can connect via the phone on the web.

Microsoft (Office Live Meeting) – can accommodate groups up to 1250 participants, minimum of 5 users required; Web Access is an applet-based program running in a Java runtime environment.

IBM (Lotus Sametime Web Conferencing) – is commonly used by larger companies running a Lotus Notes/ Domino environment; on-premise hardware and software deployment model.

Netviewer (Present) – web conferences can accommodate over 100 users; no software or hardware installation required; includes streaming audio and video.

What is a podcast?

A podcast is a pre-recorded audio or video file, usually five to seven minutes in length, which can be downloaded and played on one of the many inexpensive podcast players in use today. Anyone can create a podcast and many people are creating their own podcasts to share their creative content with others.

Well-produced podcasts offer real content on virtually any subject, and people have been subscribing to them for years. They can come in any number of formats, lengths, or styles. Talk-based podcasts are produced in several different formats: 1) single host, 2) multi-host, 3) interview-based, and 4) review-style.

There are both benefits and drawbacks to each of these approaches, but testing results indicate that listeners react most favorably to the multi-host format.

Other podcasts may offer original musical content; others still may cover news, politics, movie reviews, and the always popular entertainment topics. Podcasters enjoy talking about their passions and sharing them with other people of similar interests. This radio-like method of one-way communication is a very compelling and convenient channel for wide scale information sharing.

Many major media companies offer their own syndicated podcast programs. Forbes, BusinessWeek Online, Rush Limbaugh, ESPN, National Public Radio, USAToday, the New York Times, and thousands of other media sources produce daily podcasts that can subscribed to for free or by paid subscription

Essentially, all of the equipment needed to create a podcast is a computer with a broadband internet connection, a microphone, a video camera (optional) and some free sound editing software (also optional). Podcasts are created using one of a number of file formats including audio (MP3, M4a and WAV) or video (MP4, M4V, WMV, AVI, and MOV).

Once your podcast has been created, there are as many as one hundred different podcast directories it can be uploaded to for distribution. The Apple iTunes Store is, by far, the most important directory and can give your podcast content the kind of massive exposure it would difficult to get elsewhere as easily.

The podcast files can be manually selected for download by consumers, or can be downloaded automatically over the internet and stored on their podcast players for later playback by subscribing to what is called an RSS (Really Simple Syndication) feed. It's also referred to as a podcast feed. A software program called a podcast aggregator, or podcatcher, is used to subscribe to the RSS feed. The podcatcher checks the feed regularly for any new podcasts that have been added, and when it finds some they're downloaded to your podcast-capable device.

If you have a WordPress-based business website or blog, you're most likely already publishing an RSS feed automatically. Any podcasts or blog posts added to your website will be picked up by the feed and will be made available to anyone who chooses to subscribe.

Today there are over a thousand different podcatcher applications available for people to use on their PCs and laptops, and some are designed to work exclusively on mobile devices. Many podcatchers are free; others are available for a small price but come equipped with extra features and dozens of feeds already pre-loaded. The most popular readers include iTunes, FireAnt, Juice and Doppler.

Why use podcasts?

Podcasting can offer some significant benefits to a chiropractic practice, namely:

- It's easy to establish your own unique internet personality and build upon the K-L-T factor important to both current and prospective customers.
- Over time, podcasts can help bolster your professional reputation as an expert in the chiropractic niche as you gradually create and publish more content;
- Podcasting will help further distinguish you from your competitors (who most certainly are not podcasting);
- As your audience listens to your podcasts and shares them with others, your website will see increased traffic as more potential patients visit it;

- Podcasts can be monetized using paid sponsorships, placing advertisements in podcast transcripts, podcasting using a paid subscription model, and numerous other methods.

BlogTalkRadio

BlogTalkRadio.com is a webcast / podcast application hybrid that you may find interesting. After opening a BTR account, you can schedule your own talk shows through the BTR website and then have live guests call into them when you're "on the air". Not long after your segment ends, BTR automatically creates an audio podcast for you and stores it in your BTR podcast library where it can be downloaded anytime on demand as an MP3 file.

BTR offers several different levels of membership. A basic free account allows you to record up to 30-minute broadcast segments that you can schedule whenever you want except during their "prime time" hours of 7 – 11pm EST. BTR also provides (toll) call-in telephone numbers for both the host and the guests to use during the show. (Skype, an internet phone application, can also be integrated with your BTR account instead of using BTR's toll numbers.)

Recommendation

Yes, choose whichever medium best suits your preferences. I would suggest starting with a basic BlogTalkRadio account to get the feel of podcasting and to take advantage of their automated podcast production process. Integrate the content of the podcasts you produce into your overall internet marketing program. The time and material costs involved are negligible, particularly if you have existing content you can re-purpose. Leverage existing chiropractic studies you've been involved with, papers or articles you or others have written, or other chiropractic content you or others have produced by turning them into either individual or serialized podcasts. Make your "general information" podcasts available for free download on both your primary website and on Apple iTunes. Once you have become comfortable creating podcasts, you can explore monetizing certain categories of your podcast content through syndication across other podcasting directories.

Not only will your current and prospective patients benefit from the information you share with them using a format many are familiar with, but your own professional credentials will further benefit by virtue of being seen increasingly as an expert in your particular chiropractic discipline.

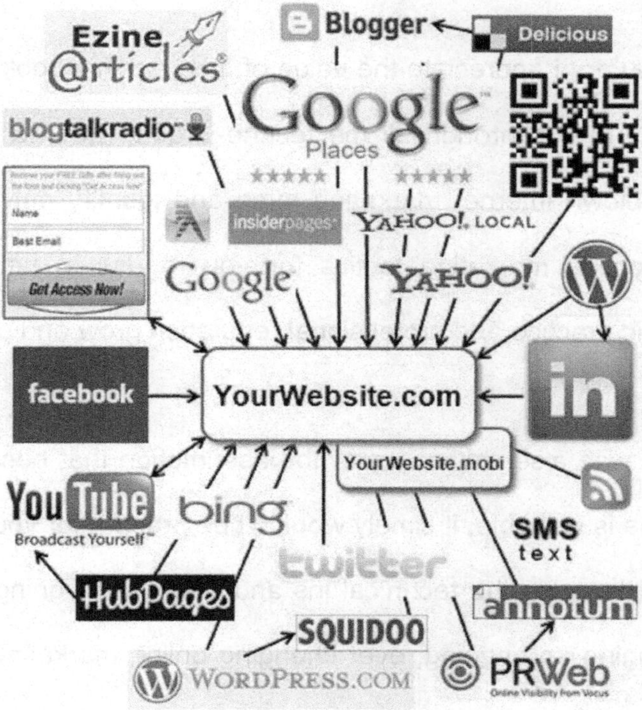

Fig. 13.1 – Add BlogTalkRadio to your ever-broadening online marketing universe.

Chapter 14 – Where To Go From Here

Just as you do, I appreciate the value of time, so this book has been an attempt to cut through all the techno-jargon, "how to" minutiae, and over-blown internet marketing hype and identify only the most effective online marketing tactics for you to use in helping your chiropractic practice and professional reputation grow and prosper.

This book was also written under the assumption that because your limited time is valuable, it simply wouldn't be prudent for you to spend much of it learning the technical ins and outs of designing, creating and managing an ongoing, ever changing online marketing program for your practice. My two hopes, then, are that this book 1) has helped improve your understanding of exactly what internet marketing is all about and how it can help your business, and 2) has now made you a better informed business owner comfortable discussing strategy and implementation with a qualified internet marketing service provider who can help you.

If you're interested in implementing any of the internet marketing strategies covered here, **NetCentricity** is a full-service internet marketing and consulting company experienced in developing highly effective online marketing programs for businesses just like yours.

Our areas of expertise include custom web and mobile web design, SEO, email / video / social media / SMS marketing, Google Places optimization, reputation management and recovery, graphic design, and other related services. For more information, feel free to contact us at **info@netcentricity.com** or by calling **(800) 519-5391**.

I hope you have found the information presented here to be useful and of value to you. Thanks very much for reading, and you have my best wishes for continued success in all of your business endeavors!

Steve Houston

NetCentricity LC

Appendix A – More Marketing Tips for Chiropractic Professionals

1. Some of your most effective internet marketing strategies rely on using the email addresses and cell phone numbers of both your current clients and prospects. Make every effort to obtain both whenever you have the opportunity, but at least make sure you acquire email addresses. Be sure to post all the appropriate data and privacy disclosures.

2. Conversely, ensure your clients and prospects have easy access to all of *your* contact information, including your office's main telephone number, emergency telephone number, main email address, street address of your office, your practice's Facebook page name, YouTube channel name, and Twitter "handle" or name. Maps should be included wherever possible.

3. The two most important online marketing trends really beginning to take off right now and which portend to be significant game-changers themselves over the next five years are **geo-targeted marketing** and **mobile marketing**. Be sure that your internet marketing program is paying appropriate attention to geo-targeting using Google Places as its focal point. New geo-location services will also drive mobile platform growth as local search via smartphone continues to explode and play an increasingly large part of the overall search volume.

4. Allowing for the many advantages that online marketing now has over the more traditional forms of advertising such as direct mail, Yellow Pages book ads, newspaper ads, and television and radio media buys, that's not to say that some of these older channels aren't still appropriate candidates to consider for use in your overall marketing plan. Even online giants Google and Facebook recognize that a blended marketing approach using a variety of channels yields the best results as they themselves also commonly use direct mail, magazine ads, and other offline methods to further broaden their marketing reach.

5. Automate the distribution of forms and other paperwork through your web site by allowing patients to download them and have them filled out in advance of their appointment, saving time and money. In addition to the sharing of free *digital* content mentioned in earlier chapters to encourage K-L-T, downloads of free *printable* content that you may want to consider offering include brochures, chiropractic health guides, new treatment or product information, and even chiropractic-related coloring pages for children.

6. Welcome visitors to your website with a pre-recorded personal greeting using an audio file that plays automatically when they arrive on your homepage. This helps personalize you even more to your prospects. Be expressive, personal, and brief.

7. Asking patients for referrals may make many chiropractors feel uneasy, but it will help you expand your client base. Many patients assume that you're too busy to take on new clients and may not give any thought to referring you to their family and friends. A simple reminder at the end of the office visit, or a business card slipped into their hand before leaving, is all that it really takes.

8. At the end of every piece of promotional content you produce, be sure to include a "call to action" (CTA) for the reader. Remove all guesswork they may have about what comes next and tell them exactly what to do - call your office to make an appointment, visit your website to download more information, etc. If they have found your information useful and compelling, this is a great opportunity to "convert" them from being a prospect into becoming an actual client.

9. To improve patient loyalty and increase referrals, consider implementing a customer rewards program for your practice. Reward programs typically offer prizes, discounts, or other types of incentives. Offer rewards relevant to your particular chiropractic discipline and make it easy for your clients to participate in the program. Fully leverage your social media assets to help promote your rewards program, and make the rewards program highly visible on all your other online assets.

10. Don't neglect ongoing "customer relationship" training for your office staff. A large percentage of negative online reviews and ratings are related to how poorly the client perceived their treatment to be by the staff, not necessarily the chiropractic treatment delivered. Sensitivity and compassion demonstrated by your staff - making your patients feel welcome and appreciated – plays a critical role in new patient acquisitions, long-term retention, and new patient referrals.

Appendix B - Chapter Highlights

Chapter 1 **Internet Inception**	Adding netcentricity to your business' marketing program is an imperative today Your patients and prospects expect you to engage online with them in the arenas of *their* choice Knowing your average patient's Customer Lifetime Value is important to calculating your marketing budget's ROI It's all relationship marketing now…and today's consumer calls the shots Your competitors are actively in the game…aren't you yet?
Chapter 2 **The Humble Website**	Your primary business website is your "money" site It's the most valuable piece of online real estate that you own and control It should be designed for new visitors and should serve to inspire Know-Like-Trust in prospective clients

	Your web site should have an email address capture form on every one of its web pages Use WordPress content management software (CMS) as your website's programming platform Blog about your hobbies, not your chiropractic practice Give your mobile visitors a mobile-friendly alternative to your main web site
Chapter 3 **Search Engines 101**	Your website earns high search engine rankings primarily through keyword relevancy and web site authority Both on-page and off-page optimization are key SEO requirements for any online asset Google's updates to its search algorithms change website rankings over time Accumulating backlinks to your website from relevant, high-authority websites is critical to earning higher search engine rankings

	An ongoing SEO program to needed to maintain your website's high rankings in Google and the other search engines
Chapter 4 **Google AdWords PPC**	Free, organic search engine traffic should be the primary focus of your internet marketing program A Google's AdWords "pay per click" (PPC) campaign can help drive additional targeted traffic to your website when it makes sense for your marketing budget "Split testing" is a critical element in any successful PPC campaign and shouldn't be overlooked
Chapter 5 **Google Places, et al**	A Google Places is *the* premier online business directory listing today Your Google Places listing, when tightly optimized with your primary website, will help you dominate page 1 of Google's search results for your chosen keywords You can claim and optimize dozens of other (free and paid) online business directory listings, using them to boost

	your own site's relevance and authority Listing citations should be complete and consistent with each other
Chapter 6 **Social Proof**	Testimonials, customer reviews, and five-star ratings are powerful marketing tools that are called "social proof"; it plays a part in 65% of all buying decisions Negative online reviews and ratings can deflect up to 90% of all potential clients away from your business and directly to your competitors You have to actively engage with your customers online to be able to manage your professional online reputation Implement a formal patient survey process and take control of your own online reviews and ratings, but use a 3rd party to administer it Before using patient testimonials, check to see if their use in marketing your chiropractic practice would violate your state's chiropractic licensing board guidelines

Chapter 7 **Reputation Mgmt.**	The advent of customer reviews being publicly posted on websites has spawned a new B2B service – online reputation management Reputation management is an ongoing process that proactively monitors your business / brand and attempts to de-fuse any attack, complaint or provocation Reputation recovery is an all-out SEO blitz program that attempts to displace negative ratings or comments with positive reviews in a search engine results page (SERP) Once your online reputation has been damaged, it will require a difficult, costly, and lengthy effort to re-build it
Chapter 8 **Social Media**	Social media is where your prospective customers are, so go meet them there Facebook is the largest online social community, and where many companies are rushing to set up their Facebook "Pages" for their businesses / brands You should establish a Facebook Page

	for your own chiropractic practice, as this will give you a way to gain exposure for it by sharing information and letting visitors get to know you You use the relationships you establish online in social media sites not to sell with, but to earn enough people's K-L-T to drive interested traffic back to your website where the sale (or "conversion") takes place You can run formal promotions on your Facebook business Page but there are strict guidelines that must be followed Twitter is another social media channel for connecting with your clients, but not for overt marketing purposes You should also get established on LinkedIn to find and take advantage of networking and B2B joint venture opportunities with your professional colleagues
Chapter 9 **Email Marketing**	Email marketing is an easy and cost-effective way to nurture your relationship with existing and potential clients

	A series of emails, newsletters, brochures or other types of interesting, valuable content should be periodically sent out via email autoresponders to your email "opt in" list Make sure your email opt-in form is prominently located throughout your web site. Your email lists will become some of your business' most valuable income-producing assets "The money is in the list."
Chapter 10 **Video Marketing**	Video marketing is a highly effective communication channel for helping prospects become aware of you and your professional services Short (3 or 4 minutes length) reality-style videos appeal to most viewers Inexpensive to produce, a series of videos relevant to your business can be hosted on your own YouTube video channel

	Google loves videos because they help convey authority, so it rewards them with high listings in their search results Videos are easily syndicated to other popular video sharing sites, increasing their exposure and marketing value to your business Even if no other effort is made, at least take some simple videos of your business with a smartphone and post them on your Google Places page and website for the authority value
Chapter 11 **QR Codes**	QR ("quick response") codes can be a useful tool for creating additional "scannable" links between your web properties QR code use appeals to a younger customer demographic, one equipped with a smartphone enabled with QR code scanning software You can easily integrate QR codes into your various types of marketing content, making it easier for prospects to find your website or other types of information

Chapter 12 **SMS / Text Messaging**	96% of all cell phones in use today have SMS (text) messaging capability The "open" rates on text messaging is strikingly high, mostly because text messages usually come from a limited number of acquaintances Use "implicit" or "explicit" acquisition methods to build your list of cell phone numbers Use SMS not as a overt marketing channel for your patients but as a value-added support service offered by your chiropractic practice
Chapter 13 **Webcasts, Webinars and Podcasts**	You can take your marketing program to the next level by hosting live events like webinars, webcasts or podcasts that instantly boost your K-L-T factor Any of these events (live or recorded) can be hosted from your own office using a PC with a broadband internet connection and an external microphone Recorded content can be offered for free download to your clients and prospects in

	a variety of media types (audio CD, MP3 audio files, MP4 videos, written transcripts, etc.) BlogTalkRadio.com is be a good way to get a start with broadcasting; it can also help you produce re-usable content for wider distribution
Chapter 14 **Where To Go From Here**	Use this book to acquaint yourself with the newest internet marketing principles available today Unless you want to spend the time to do it yourself, contract out the development, implementation, & on-going management of your internet marketing program to qualified professionals

Made in United States
Orlando, FL
04 November 2026

90200404R00085